"A book is a mirror: if an ass peers
into it, you cannot expect an apostle
to look out."

- Lichtenberg

Produced in Ireland by Blackwater Press,
Broomhill Business Park, Tallaght, Dublin

ISBN 0861215303 (HBK)
ISBN 0861215508 (PBK)

DEAR JOHN

THE JOHN MACKAY LETTERS

BLACKWATER PRESS

John Mackay was born in Dublin in 1950.

A compulsive correspondent and an entrepreneur by instinct, he describes his current employment status as "between challenges".

Deeply committed to the nuclear family, he has structured his household as a limited liability company, with himself as chief executive and chairman of Mackay plc, his wife Dympna as company secretary, and his son Tobias (22) and daughter Susie (17) as non-executive directors.

A contemporary Irish patriot with roots in several counties, he is cosmopolitan by inclination and has lived in both England and the United States.

Where others see conflict and confusion in his personal philosophy, this pragmatic ideological chameleon sees no contradiction: "I am what I am," he says.

Dedication: *To Nessie*

Salem Court
Maxwell Road
Dublin 6

Professor Helmut Schlesinger
President
Bundesbank
Bonn
Germany

10 August 1993

Dear Dr Schlesinger,

Following the devaluation of the IR£, you are reported to have said
that the difference between the Irish Central Bank and the Irish soccer
team is that the Irish soccer team has more foreign reserves.

Dr Schlesinger, I too despair of the Irish economy and the political
clowns who run the show, so, when I heard that you were retiring from
the Bundesbank, I thought I should ask you to consider becoming Governor
of the Irish Central Bank.

After discussions with my wife Dympna, we concluded that running the
Irish economy need not be a full-time job for a man of your ability, but
rather a handy "nixer" or part-time job where you could "moonlight" on
your retirement, just as some pensioners become nightwatchmen or carpark
attendants. What do you think?

While we have your attention, could we also seek your advice on another
proposal? I am currently unemployed (though seeking entrepreneurial
challenges) and, due to the notoriously volatile nature of the punt –
and my deep personal distrust of Irish financial institutions – I would
like to open a Current Account with the Bundesbank and have my dole
payments paid directly into that account in deutschmarks.

Can this be arranged, Dr Schlesinger? Please send me the necessary
forms. I enclose IR£5 to cover postage and administrative costs.

Yours sincerely,

John Mackay

Mr John Mackay

PS Could you also send Dympna and I a signed photo of yourself? We have
always admired your Euro-fiscal stewardship.

Helmut Franz Lilienweyer

MANFRED KIESEL
LEITER DES BÜROS DES PRÄSIDENTEN
DER DEUTSCHEN BUNDESBANK

D-6000 FRANKFURT AM MAIN 50
WILHELM-EPSTEIN-STRASSE 14
TELEFON (069) 1 58 22 21

August 27, 1993

Mrs Dympna Mackay and
Mr John Mackay

Salem Court
Maxwell Road

Dublin 6

Irland

Dear Mrs Mackay, dear Mr Mackay,

Thank you very much for your whimsical letter of August 10, 1993
to President Schlesinger. I must ask for your understanding that I
cannot comment on your assessment of the economic situation in
Ireland. On behalf of President Schlesinger, I would like to thank
you for the friendly words you found for him. However, I must
return the IR£ 5.-- postal order you had enclosed. It is not
possible to open private accounts at the Deutsche Bundesbank.

The signed photograph of President Schlesinger you requested is
enclosed.

Yours sincerely,

Salem Court
Maxwell Road
Dublin 6

17 Feb 1993

Albert Reynolds
Taoiseach
Leinster House
Dublin 2

Dear Taoiseach,

Firstly, many congratulations on retaining the top spot against the odds. As O'Malley sulked and Bruton sank, your masterly £8 billion Eurodeal spat in the face of a visionless electorate's snub. Your Spring-loaded return means national recovery is in sight.

I, like you, understand people. May I be so bold as to advise that you refuse to budge from your approachable "howaya" image? Though the liberals may smirk and the media gurus shrink with embarrassment, the Maastricht poll showed clearly that we do not want an "intellectual" Taoiseach who "has all the answers".

As an Irish John Major - on the face of it nondescript, yet startlingly effective - you have set the winning tone for the nineties. Consensus "Reynoldsite" politics may seem less dramatic than the "decisive" Thatcher/ Haughey variety, yet you have stayed on top by staying out of sight and doing the job. Let them call you the invisible man, but when the bandages are removed and national salvation complete, they will understand. Say no more.

I was hoping that you could, as a true "man-of-the-people" Taoiseach, give me some small advice on a matter unrelated to politics, but with which I understand you have some commercial familiarity. My daughter Susie has a beautiful spaniel puppy which refuses to eat her dogfood unless it is given to her on one of the family's dinner plates.

Is it possible to buy anywhere in Ireland a dogfood bowl modelled as a willow pattern plexiglass dinner plate? No pet stores I have visited stock them, and the owners all say they do not believe there would be sufficient demand to justify making them. Perhaps the IDA might look into it. I know this is probably too trivial a matter to concern you personally, but maybe you could send the query "down the line" to a suitable civil servant. Max-a-million!

Yours sincerely,

John Mackay

Mr John Mackay

PS Please find enclosed a token donation to the Party coffers. Also, what arrangements should I make to contribute regularly to the Party by standing order?

_26_ February, 1993.

Oifig an Taoisigh
Office of the Taoiseach

Mr. John Mackay,

Salem Court,
Maxwell Road,
Dublin 6.

Dear John,

Many thanks for your recent letter and kind sentiments contained therein.

I will certainly make enquiries with the IDA regarding the question of dogfood bowls modelled as dinner plates and I will write to you when I have some news.

I also wish to acknowledge receipt of the £5.00 postal order which you forwarded to the Fianna Fail party and I have asked Mr. Pat Farrell, General Secretary, Fianna Fail to contact you regarding future arrangements if you should wish to contribute.

Best wishes for the future.

Yours sincerely,

Albert Reynolds
Taoiseach.

Salem Court
Maxwell Road
Dublin 6

3 June 1993

Bishop Joseph Duffy
Bishop of Clogher
County Monaghan

Dear Bishop Duffy,

I read that your house – a spacious Georgian mansion with billiards room, wine cellar and two acre secluded garden – is worth a quarter of a million pounds, and that a sample dozen of your episcopal colleagues live in estates collectively costing over three million.

Here's a thought that struck my wife Dympna: "They should sell the houses, buy cheaper ones, and give the balance to the poor!"

"Quiet, woman." I explained, "The Bishops are good and holy men. If that was the right thing to do, they would have done so ages ago".

As one does in such instances, we resorted to the Family Bible.

"Mark 10:42" I said. "Those who rule over the Gentiles lord it over them, and their great men exercise authority over them".

"Mark 10:43" retorted Dympna. "But it shall not be so among you; whoever would be great among you must be your servant, and whoever would be first among you must be slave of all".

"Matthew 20:30" I countered. "You (the Disciples – the FUTURE BISHOPS) shall sit on twelve thrones judging the twelve tribes".

"Tell that to Mother Teresa" said Dympna. I was flummoxed.

Your Grace, I still think you're right and she's wrong, but the debate remains ongoing. You're always very good on the telly as the spokesman for the Bishops; perhaps you could oblige me with a few well-chosen words to settle the issue once and for all.

Yours sincerely,

John Mackay

Mr John Mackay

The Bishop's House
Monaghan

8 June 1993

Mr John Mackay,

Salem Court,
Maxwell Road,
Dublin 6.

Dear Mr Mackay,

Thank you for your wise and witty letter.

Your good wife may be relieved to know that there has not been a
wine cellar in this house in living memory,certainly not since 1943.
The billiards room is the Diocesan library since 1970 and a number of
the bed rooms are taken up with Diocesan offices. As the house is
attached to the Cathedral grounds it is anything but secluded and
could realistically be sold only in the event of the Cathedral also
being put on the open market.

Ultimately the local people who keep this place will decide its
destiny. A few years ago when a bubgalow was sold on the edge of the
grounds where the retired bishop had lived, there was agro.

However, it is obviously the principle of clerics owning or having
the use of property which is bothering you. I dont either own or
have the use of this house for my day. My predecessor spent the last
years of his life in a home for the elderly funded largely by the
Health Board and with no privileges not enjoyed by non-paying
residents. As I keep reminding the priests, it's the life-style that
counts, not where you live. Some of us live in beautiful houses; others
in houses below the average of their parishioners. Before coming here
I lived in one of the latter. All things considered, the ideal is
a modicum of decent comfort which even Mother Teresa enjoys.

Thnks for your interest and sorry the typing is not better. I need
a word-processor ?

Yours sincerely,

+Joseph Duffy

+Joseph Duffy

Dawson Stelfox
99 Dunmurray Lane
Belfast BT1 79JU
Northern Ireland

Salem Court
Maxwell Road
Dublin 6

17 August 1993

Dear Mr Stelfox,

Can you find it in your heart to forgive an ungrateful nation that has already consigned your becoming the first Irishman to conquer Mount Everest to the trivia of a Dublin pub quiz?

I believe your achievement is no less historic than man's first steps on the moon. Your climbing boot on the peak of Everest was a small step for a mountaineer, but a giant leap for Irishmankind.

After the offending pub quiz, I and a few friends got to discussing what would constitute a suitable monument to your herculean efforts. We settled on the concept of commissioning a statue of yourself and US moon-man Neil Armstrong, perhaps flanked by your expedition deputies Buzz Aldrin and Frank Nugent, to be sited outside the American Embassy in Dublin's Ballsbridge.

Recognising that this would cost a packet, we then considered some imaginative fund-raising schemes. Dawson, could you climb Dublin's tallest building, Liberty Hall? It is a glass edifice, so crampons and an ice-pick would be out - even in Winter!

Instead you could wear a Spiderman suit and attach rubber suckers to your hands and feet - it would attract both enormous publicity and commensurate funds for the statue. What do you think?

I'm sure it would be okay with the Irish Congress of Trade Unions, who own the building - and the American Ambassador could greet you at the top, where you could intertwine the Tricolour with the Stars and Stripes for maximum pictorial impact.

Please let us know what you think - and again, congratulations on reaching the top of the world!

Yours sincerely,

John Mackay

John Mackay

LEADER: DAWSON STELFOX, 99 DUNMURRY LANE BELFAST BT17 9JU TEL: (084) 622 019
DEPUTY LEADER: FRANK NUGENT, 151 GLENMAROON RD. DUBLIN 20. TEL: (01) 626 95 80

MOUNT EVEREST

FIRST IRISH EXPEDITION

PATRON: SIR EDMUND HILLARY

John Mackay
Salem Court
Maxwell Road
Dublin 6

26th August 1993

Dear John,

Thank you for your entertaining letter.

One of the more amusing side effects of the trip has been the ability of many people, not just pub quiz participants, to spell my name correctly - previously a source of much error and hilarity.

Your ideas are worthy of the most ambitious PR agent but I don't think I could bring myself to climbing up anything in a Spiderman outfit.

Come along to one of our Dublin slide shows (Sep 9th and 10th, UCD, tickets from the Great Outdoors, Chatham Street, Dublin) and make yourself known.

Yours,

1993

Salem Court
Maxwell Road
Dublin 6

2 March 1993

Mr Larry Goodman,
Goodman International,
Ardee,
County Louth

Dear Mr Goodman,

Intellectual arrogance and chronic confusion have been hallmarks of the 1990s, but nothing, I repeat nothing, has so graphically displayed the bankruptcy of our national political herd than the so-called Beef Tribunal. It makes me feel ashamed to be Irish.

You were born in humble circumstances to a modest family in a disadvantaged area of north Louth, eschewed formal education for a grounding course in the University of Shrewd Deals, and went on to become the biggest and most successful beef exporter in Europe.

Now a motley coalition of fundamentalist boy-scouts ranging the spectrum from PD to Labour, with the part of Violet Elizabeth Bott played by the you-know Harney, and the hydra-headed diaspora of Moscow Central in the persons of Dick and Probiscus, hope to bury you in their Luddite dug-out.

It is time to say: Enough and no more. Whatever aids, grants and subsidies you got from the bureaucrats of Brussels were willingly given by the VAT-payers of the Europe. Other nations were happy to fund you. They know how things work. But we, in our isolationist purity, know better. We must bring you down to our gutter level.

No longer! A few of us here believe it is time to strike a balance, and a blow or two for the little guy in the form of a planned Public Campaign for Economic Common Sense. Like any struggle, it will not be easy, but then you, Mr Goodman, have never taken the motorway when there is a lonely track as an alternative.

I enclose £5, a token, to encourage you to join a quest for economic justice and job creation. It is your headage payment for teaming up and turning out. We would welcome your advice and support.

Yours sincerely,

John Mackay

Mr John Mackay

Mr John Mackay

Salem Court
Maxwell Road
DUBLIN 6

6 April 1993

Dear Mr Mackay

Many thanks for your recent letter, which I think reflects the feelings of a large percentage of the population.

Whilst I would like to become involved in your ideas for a campaign to seek economic justice and job creation, as you are no doubt aware, I am presently in the throes of the Tribunal after which I would hope to devote all my energies into trying to recoup the damage done to our Group in the Dail, by the Gulf War, and finally the Tribunal, which unfortunately will leave me little time for anything else.

I am returning your Postal Order so that you can put it to the use it was intended for; in the meantime I really appreciate your asking me to become involved in your project, and would like to take this opportunity of wishing you every success with it.

Yours sincerely

L J Goodman
Chief Executive

14 Castle Street, Ardee, Co. Louth, Ireland.
Tel. 041-53754. Telex: 43081. Fax. 041-53064
Goodman International. Reg. No. 96842

Salem Court
Maxwell Road
Dublin 6

23 Feb 1993

Father Pat Buckley
The Oratory
Princes Gardens
Larne, County Antrim

Dear Father Buckley,

Congratulations on your forthright defence of truth, and attack on hypocrisy, within the Roman Catholic Church and your razor-sharp willingness to translate consience into action. Your unsubstantiated allegations of last year that Bishop Casey was not alone among the hierarchy in his foibles caused some hot public flushes in at least two prominant prelates!

However, it is about the intrinsically related moral dilemna of the non-clerical partners in such relationships that I write to you for advice. I am not a priest, yet I have for over eleven years been involved in an ongoing once-every-two-months sexual indiscretion with (not always at the same time) an ex-priest, a prominent Dublin businesswoman, a professional footballer with a penchant for green, and two beautiful nuns who teach in a school attended by a daughter of my cousin.

We each know what we are doing is wrong but, much like the good Bishop of Galway and the other clergy to whom you have refered, we simply cannot help ourselves. We have limited the extent of our sin by refusing to use artificial contraceptives, relying instead on the papally-preferred rhythm and withdrawal methods (which have thankfully - or as we like to joke, miraculously - proved successful so far).

However, the recent secret visit home of Bishop Casey has reminded us yet again of the very real dangers of pregnancy, and we have decided to turn to your good self for some value-free moral guidance. Should we start to use artificial contraceptives, which are available through record shops in Dublin? Should we continue with the rhythm and withdrawal methods? Or should we simply try to get together less often, or even stop altogether?

Please do not ask us to join the clerical sex-partners group you are forming, as we are not yet ready for such a traumatic step.

Yours sincerely,

John Mackay

Mr John Mackay

THE ORATORY
Princes Gardens,
Larne,
Co. Antrim,
Northern Ireland
BT40 1RQ

Fr. Pat Buckley

26 / 2 / 93

Dear John,

Thank you for your most unusual letter. Whatever else we might say, we must admire your unbounded energies!

Your main problem seems to be the contraceptive one. There is an old Celtic potion to prevent conception. It was given to me by a rural Archdeacon.

You get a large saucepan and add:
The heart of a head of cabbage
The two hind legs of a hare caught in March
2 ozs black and 1 1/2 ozs white pudding
1/2 pint of Irish Mist whiskey
4 pints of spring water
2 pigs testicles
1/2 pint of dry altar wine

Boil the above for 2 hours. Strain and store the liquid in a bottle. Take two teaspoons last thing at night and first thing in the morning. After one month, there is no chance of conception - even for a woman.

I wish you well in your active life.

Best wishes,

Pat Buckley

Dr Garret FitzGerald
30 Palmerstown Road
Dublin 6

Salem Court
Maxwell Road
Dublin 6

17 Feb 1993

Dear Dr FitzGerald,

Frankly, though a lifelong Fine Gael voter, I never felt comfortable with you as Taoiseach - guiding a nation through the traumas of the post-industrial era requires a level of mental dexterity somewhat inconsistent with putting on odd shoes. Jobs and law and order were always higher up my agenda than promulgating the benefits of marriage breakdown and condom vending machines.

In retrospect, however, it is clear that I was wrong, wrong, wrong. Your leadership was the engine that fired Fine Gael's rise to its electoral apex. Today, as crime rates soar and the currency sinks, neither of your successors have been able to wrest the levers of power from a never more directionless Fianna Fail party.

I was very impressed with John Bruton's policy of combining exciting new ideas on job creation with the traditional reactionary law and order policies Ireland so badly needs. However, Mr Bruton is unfortunately seen as something of a political buffoon, much as Alan Dukes was unfairly seen as a rather tall schoolboy visiting the Dail. Here's the nub. As the country descends further into chaos, we have yet to be offered the "dream ticket" of Bruton / Dukes policies under a Fitzgerald leadership - a statesmanlike onslaught on jobs and crime, sold effectively by your personal stature and unrivalled charisma.

Having recently returned to Ireland, I have decided to join Fine Gael. I am a man of ideas, some of which may be useful to the party. As an example, along with some colleagues, I am contemplating launching a non-party-political "Bring Back Garret" campaign. I must stress that this would happen outside the party "machine" and would in no way be seen to reflect on the current Bruton leadership. We have a substantial nest-egg available for promotion etc, and the campaign would not be a drain on the party coffers.

Would we need your formal endorsement, or should that come after the launch? Please let us know. At least, please let us know that you have not definitively closed the door on such a return to power.

Yours sincerely,

John Mackay

Mr John Mackay

PS I have started to read your excellent though lengthy biography, which I hope to finish some time this year. When I do, would you like me to write to you with some constructive criticism?

DR. GARRET FITZGERALD

30 Palmerston Road,
Rathmines,
Dublin 6.
Telephone: 962506
Fax: 962126

1st March 1993

Mr. John Mackay,

Salem Court,
Maxwell Road,
Dublin, 6.

Dear Mr. Mackay,

Thank you for your letter dated 17th February.

I gratefully appreciate the terms in your letter - all the more so because of your earlier doubts! However, I am afraid that your idea of a "Bring back Garret" campaign is simply not on. I am now aged 67 and have to take things easier because of a heart problem. There are no circumstances under which I would consider any further involvement in politics. The best contribution I can make now is from a position of relative detachment outside the system.

Sorry about this!

I am interested to hear that you are reading my biography and would welcome any constructive criticism.

Kind regards.

Yours sincerely,

Dr. Garret FitzGerald

p.s.   I don't agree with you about mental dexterity and odd shoes!

Salem Court
Maxwell Road
Dublin 6

24 September 1993

Professor David Norris
Seanad Eireann
Leinster House
Kildare Street
Dublin 2

Dear Professor Norris,

My wife Dympna and I are having some friends in over the Christmas for a few drinks and would like our guests to leave with a surprise present. Rather than some gift-wrapped copies of the latest Seamus Heaney offering, we believe the memory of a performance of your one-man-show "Ja, Ja, James Joyce" would be an experience they could tell their friends about — and enhance the MacKay's reputation as imaginative hosts.

Do you do house parties? We envisage clearing the end of the drawing room to create a stage, with a screen erected where you could do your quick costume changes, and a stereo providing mood and background music operated by our son, Toby, who would also act as stage manager.

Professor Norris, we realise it is impossible to put a price on art, but we also know that quality doesn't come cheap. A three-figure fee will not surprise us, a taxi would ferry you door-to-door.

You could also bring a friend and both of you could eat at our table just like the other guests, who would not be told you were receiving money for attending - perhaps you could intimate to them that we had met at some literary academic forum.

We were thinking of St Stephen's Day, and an early reply would be appreciated so that we can prepare our invitations.

Yours sincerely,

John Mackay

Mr John Mackay

John Mackay, Esq.,

Salem Court,
Maxwell Road,
Dublin 6.

18 October 1993

Dear Mr. Mackay,

Thank you very much for your letter and kind invitation which I received on my return from abroad. In fact I really only do the Joyce One Man Show for charity and am rather looking forward to a rest at the Christmas period as I will be putting in a pretty gruelling time before that trying to finish writing a book, editing another, completing a play, starting on a twelve part T.V. series about Joyce, hoofing it on stage with Tony Kenny in 'Side by Side by Sondheim' as well as trying to keep going in the Senate and Trinity. I hope in the circumstances you will excuse me. I am sure you will find somebody who would grace your Christmas festivities at what sounds like a simply splendid evening.

With best wishes.

Yours sincerely,

Senator David Norris

Salem Court
Maxwell Road
Dublin 6

11 June 1993

The Treasurer
Fianna Fail
Mount Street
Dublin 1

Dear Treasurer,

It is hardly a classified secret that your party is tottering on the brink of financial ruin — if not ideological bankruptcy — so I'll not waste either of our time with coy euphemisms. I have returned from "off-shore" where I made a lot and brushed shoulders with titled folk. I liked the grovelling of poorer people and the respect the aristocracy usually gives to "eccentric" men of means.

But, in my case, you can forget the "eccentric" bit: I did it to get preferential treatment, good seats in restuarants and my photograph in the newspapers with government ministers or pop stars attending charity functions. And so to business, and let me be frank; I write to you not out of ideological motivation, but because you are in government and therefore able to deliver what I want.

I believe that you should introduce an Irish honours system, and in a manner that enables those who contribute to your party to lead the queue. Starting on the "green field site" that is this young republic, the titles could be formally "auctioned" by whichever parties are in power; it is the republican and democratic way.

The titles themselves could be structured on the usual monarchist model; dukes and barons etc. For years I have called my wife Dympna "the Duchess". She was a good looker in her day but time and a fondness for Belgian chocolate has taken its toll. Still, a tiara, a floor length ball gown and a title would keep her happy — and when she smiles, the world is a more agreeable place.

Please outline your thoughts on the start-rate cost of a title-related contribution (i.e. a Duke, £100,000; a baronetcy £60,000, or whatever) and the timescale within which you feel you could have such a system in place. To underline my seriousness, I enclose £5 – the first of many far more substantial donations should the proposal be put in place.

Yours sincerely,

John Mackay

Mr John Mackay

Salem Court
Maxwell Road
Dublin 6

Miley and Biddy
Glenroe
c/o RTE, Donnybrook
Dublin 4

10 August 1993

Dear Miley and Biddy,

For years, you've been a shining example of the forebearance of the Irish farming family in the face of adversity. You rose early and you worked hard; you were a happy husband and wife, a model father and mother. Until last year, that is.

Suddenly Miley, this most amiable and agreeable of hibernian hunks, was transformed into a craven adulterous monster, a one-man 18th century Hell-Fire Club in a 20th century Wicklow village.

Biddy was driven to desperation and nearly into the arms of Satan himself, fecklessly flirting with infidelity, then retreating to the relative sanctuary of factory floors and Surf Automatic ads.

This is not good enough, Miley and Biddy. You're in Glenroe, not Dallas or I Claudius. So zipper up your jeans and allow the family pyjamas to be your only procreative playpen - and let Christian Ireland watch its telly of a Sunday without fear of moral corruption.

Another thing: be a smiley Miley and a giddy Biddy. Check out Home And Away, where EVERYONE smiles ALL THE TIME, whether they're happy or not. Turn Wicklow Beach into Summer Bay, and sublimate your infidelity into some harmless frolicking on the strand with a surfboard.

Or bring a bit of action into the village - DI Frank Burnside ("Oi! You! C'meeere, you little toe-rag!") is leaving The Bill. Why not snap him up for Glenroe Garda Station, and have him "sort out" some joy-riding muggers on a day-trip from Dublin?

Let Teasy win the Lotto, then have Arthur Daly come over from London, with his Minder, to con her out of her winnings. Then let Biddy team up with Inspector Morse to sort out the mystery and restore justice. And get Shay Healy and Niamh Kavanagh to update the theme music.

What do you think? Please let me know. If you can guarantee such a conversion to cheerful exciting chastity, I'll be glued in front of my box when Glenroe returns. In anticipation of a positive response, I enclose £5 to cover the cost of you sending me a signed photo of the two of you together.

Yours sincerely,

John Mackay

Mr John Mackay

Glenroe

Drama Department,
Radio Telefís Éireann,
Dublin 4,
Ireland

August 30th, 1993

Mr. John Mackay,

Salem Court,
Maxwell Road,
Dublin 6.

Dear John,

Your letter reached us just as our last row reached a crescendo.
The effect of your words has been beneficial. It left us
smiling: We needed that.

However, we cannot guarantee a "conversion to cheerful exciting
chastity" as you require, when we return to the airwaves from 26th
September. We enclose a special photograph of us and hope you
will spend many happy hours gazing fondly at it.

We return also your postal order to prove that in the face of
moral decline and corruption that we still have standards.

Enjoy the new season.

Yours sincerely,

& Biddly

X x x

Dick Spring TD
Tanaiste, Minister for Foreign Affairs
Leader, Labour Party
Office of the Tanaiste
Government Buildings
Dublin 2

Salem Court
Maxwell Road
Dublin 6

17 Feb 1993

Dear Mr Spring,

At last, under your wise and courageous stewardship, the left is a credible force in Irish politics. Even the wild men of the party – Higgins, Stagg and their ilk – have been given some sweeties to take their minds off playing Sandanistas in their sandpits of Marxist ideology. Meantime you, and those of your colleagues who live in the real world, make the real-life decisions that have revived the left and will save Ireland from the Fianna Fail which you have transformed.

Out! is socialism as an avenue for the left. In! are the sensible realities of "social democracy", and carefully cultivated strolls in the Leinster House lawns with the leaders of the larger parties. Hello! is a glossy magazine in which Kristi and you should be featured.

The task of mobilising the masses has changed now that the masses are in the minority. The first role of Labour today is to mobilise the middle classes to ensure they do not join the destitute minority. This you have done, and the people have rewarded you.

What a pity Neill Kinnock was rejected by the sceptical British electorate. While he, like you, was happy to turn socialism upside down and stamp on its head, his ranting and raving "oratorical" style lacked the subtle yet infinitely more effective "people's champion" charisma exuded by your good self in Dail Eireann.

Your clarity of purpose and sharpness of mind consistently leave opponents for dead, perhaps lulled into a false sense of complacency by your humorous "Groucho Marx" moustache. And now you are not only Tanaiste, but in reality a rotating and revolutionary Taoiseach. You are indeed a "people's champion", but a solid and reliable one, unlike the Belfast snooker ace Alex Higgins.

And so to the point: I, like you, am a modern social democrat who can spot unhelpful leftist rhetoric with my ears shut. I would be delighted to participate in your "handlers" group, to help ensure the Party stays looking forward, not backward.

Yours sincerely,

John Mackay

Mr John Mackay

PS Please find enclosed a token donation by way of indicating my commitment to the values we share – and the shares that we value!

Oifig an Tánaiste
Office of the Tánaiste

12 March, 1993

Mr. John Mackay,

Salem Court,
Maxwell Road,
Dublin 6.

Dear Mr. Mackay,

I acknowledge with thanks receipt of your recent letter and your
indication of support.

As you know we have a very difficult task on hand but we are all
committed to the implementation of the agreed Programme for
Government over the coming four years and every offer of
assistance and support in this connection is appreciated.

We will be in touch with you again in the near future.

Best wishes.

Yours sincerely

Dick Spring, T.D.
Tánaiste

LABOUR

THE LABOUR PARTY
16 Gardiner Place
Dublin 1
Tel: (01) 788411
Fax: (01) 745479

RK/pf

30th March, 1993

Mr. John McKay,

Salem Court,
Maxwell Road,
Dublin 6.

Dear John,

Thank you very much for your contribution of £5.00 to Party funds which I gratefully acknowledge.

Sally Clarke, Personal Assistant to the Party Leader Dick Spring T.D. has asked me to send you on details of our standing order scheme and I enclose a form and pre-addressed envelope. Perhaps you might like to complete the form and return it to me.

If you require any further information or a membership application form, please do not hesitate to contact me.

Yours sincerely,

Ray Kavanagh
GENERAL SECRETARY

Encl. Request for Standing Order form and pre-addressed envelope.

Post: Senator Pat Magner

Dick Spring TD
Tanaiste, Minister for Foreign Affairs
Leader, Labour Party
Office of the Tanaiste
Government Buildings
Dublin 2

Salem Court
Maxwell Road
Dublin 6

18 May 1993

Dear Mr Spring,

I wrote to you on 17 Feb and slipped you a financial donation together with an offer to involve myself in your "handlers" group. What response did I get? What appears to be a series of roneod stock replies, one from your office and one from a faceless aparatchik by name of Ray Kavanagh (is he a son of deputy Liam Kavanagh of Wicklow?)

Mr Spring, If this is the fire in the belly of Irish socialism, I am getting cold feet down below. I offer to invest my time and energy, free of charge, in your political activities and I am patronisingly fobbed off with two Dear John letters.

Perhaps I am over-reacting.

You are a busy man and you are, after all, only settling down in your job. Your American visit seems to have gone very well, with yourself and Presidents Mary and Bill starting to make the Left respectable in a land where the Centre is to the Right of Ghengis Kahn.

And so I still want to help you and I repeat my offer to join your "Think Tank". I have read a book on "lateral thinking" and have come up with the following ideas: On the "national question" - everyone in Britain and Ireland gets a new citizenship called "Bryrish". On the jobs issue - share them out. Everyone does a little less than they should and lets someone else do the bit that they aren't doing.

Please feel free to bring these ideas to the government table without prior attribution. Please also let me know if there are any other areas of policy on which you would like my suggestions.

Yours sincerely,

John Mackay

Mr John Mackay

Oifig an Tánaiste
Office of the Tánaiste

28 May 1993.

Mr. John Mackay,

Salem 'Court,
Maxwell Road,
Dublin 6.

Dear Mr. Mackay,

Thank you for your further letter of 18th May.

I had passed your correspondence to the General Secretary of the Labour Party, Ray Kavanagh (who is not a son of Deputy Liam Kavanagh) as he has overall responsibility for policy coordination. Under the terms of the new Party Constitution, the General Executive Council which met for the first time last week has been given responsibility for the production of policy material and I am sure the General Secretary would appreciate receiving from you any policy ideas which may be of assistance to the Committee in its initial stages. I am asking the General Secretary to contact you on this matter again as soon as possible.

Yours sincerely,

TÁNAISTE

Editor
Roy of the Rovers
Fleetway Publications
Greater London house
Hampstead Road
London NW1 7QQ

Salem Court
Maxwell Road
Dublin 6

9 March 1993

Dear sir,

My son Toby has recently purchased your "Roy of the Rovers Power Poster" which flies under the title "Best of British". The publication purports to represent, in full colour visual format, a football team selected from the best British players of the current game.

And what a team! Two Welsh, two Scots, seven English. Nothing wrong with that. But I write concerning your decision to select as substitutes two Republic of Ireland players – Andy Townsend, who you describe as "one of the country's leading players" and Pat "Packie" Bonner who you describe as "the ideal squad man for the Best of British team". What, you may ask, is my problem? Here's a visual clue in the form of what we in Ireland call "a map":

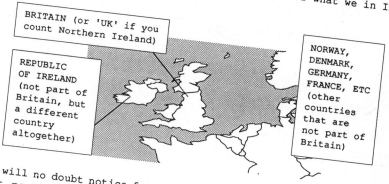

BRITAIN (or 'UK' if you count Northern Ireland)

REPUBLIC OF IRELAND (not part of Britain, but a different country altogether)

NORWAY, DENMARK, GERMANY, FRANCE, ETC (other countries that are not part of Britain)

You will no doubt notice from this "map" that the Republic of Ireland is not part of Britain, but a different country altogether. I must therefore ask you to either (a) formally apologise, by return of post, for this pre-emptive and public strike on my citizenship or (b) provide me, by return of post, with an adequate explanation. Failing this, I shall have no option but to place the matter in the hands of my solicitors, who shall extract from your good selves through due process compensation of a punitive nature.

Yours sincerely,

John Mackay

Mr John Mackay

Mr John Mackay

Salem Court
Maxwell Road
Dublin 6

22 March 1993

Dear Mr Mackay,

Thank you for your letter, which I found most interesting to read.

It is indeed a well known fact that the Republic of Ireland is not a part of Britain. But, as you are aware, the two players you make mention of are top soccer stars who earn their livings in the Premier Divisions of the English and Scottish Leagues...and for this reason they were selected as substitutes for the 'Best of British' Power Posters.

I like that reasoning and I trust you will, too!

Yours sincerely,

David Hunt, Editor: Roy of the Rovers

Salem Court
Maxwell Road
Dublin 6

17 Feb 1993

Bertie Ahern TD
Minister for Finance
Department of Finance
Merrion Street
Dublin 2

Dear Mr Ahern,

Congratulations on your masterly defence of the beleagured punt against the Euro-currency pirates. Your sensible mistrust of the Bundesbank mirrors the start of the century - Banna Strand, Casement and the same small nation waiting for help from the Hun. You have grown in financial stature as you wisely bide your leadership time.

In the meantime, I hope you can help a niece of mine, who is currently working on a UCD thesis titled "Politics And People - Electoral Interaction In The Multiple Seat STV System".

She has asked me for any "anecdotes" to illustrate the impact of our system on the valuable time of national legislators. Two examples spring to mind concerning your good self, the authenticity of which I felt I should confirm "from the horse's mouth".

Firstly, a cousin of mine who lives in Drumcondra tells me that you personally delivered Christmas greetings to your constituents on St Stephen's Day last. As my cousin joked, "What dedication - you would never see the Chancellor of the British Exchequer running around sticking handbills through letterboxes during his Christmas holidays".

Secondly, during a recent general election, a friend of mine approached you off Oxmantown Road where you were canvassing in appropriately casual "bomber jacket" and slacks. Your canvassers had been misleading voters by saying on the doorsteps that there were no health cuts being implemented by Fianna Fail! "Ah sure God love them" you explained to my friend with a laugh "they're not familiar with the details".

I would be glad if you would allow my niece to include these amusing, yet informational, anecdotes in her thesis.

Yours sincerely,

John Mackay

Mr John Mackay

PS I have enclosed a token contribution to your next election campaign. One good turn deserves another.

IRISH POSTAL ORDER - ÓRDÚ POIST
0510235
Head Office
Baile Átha Cliath
TO AN POST NOT NEGOTIABLE
02883662
£5.00

Her Majesty
Queen Elizabeth II
Buckingham Palace
The Mall
London SW1

Salem Court
Maxwell Road
Dublin 6
Republic of Ireland

11 July 1993

Your Majesty,

God save your glorious self! I was thrilled that you recently took tea with our President, the inestimable Mary Robinson. What an example in these days of crumbling moral and family values to have two working mothers having an old fashoned natter over the garden fence.

Perhaps because of the acetylene glare of publicity the get-together was not as relaxed and informal as it might have been. But I once saw you on a television documentary whisking a barbeque fork around like a short order cook and being a regular life and soul of the party.

And, I can assure Your Majesty, if you and President Robinson ever have an opportunity to get to know each other better, you will see another little known side of our lady Head of State that her office and protocol dictate must remain private.

Much has been made of our President's illustrious career as an international and constitutional lawyer, but she is also the first to "do a turn" at any private social occasion. For instance, only her intimates know that President Robinson can play "She'll Be Coming 'Round The Mountain" on the mouth organ with foot-tapping virtuosity. And her powerful contralto voice can both scale the alps of "The Power Of Love" and slip into a folksy idiom with "The Whistling Gypsy."

Her conversational skills were polished hosting an award-winning series of Tupperware parties: she was Irish Tupperware Hostess Of The Year three times, from 1981 to 1983. And for a woman of high birth and sophisticated tastes, she is as much at home sipping a humble glass of stout as nipping at an elaborately dressed Pimms cup.

Your Majesty, is it possible to get a photograph of Oneself and President Robinson together? I enclose £5 to cover the cost.

Yours sincerely,

John MacKay

Mr John MacKay

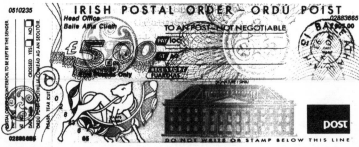

08044 009028836659 0005002 012017

BUCKINGHAM PALACE

5th August, 1993.

Dear Mr. Mackay,

I am commanded by The Queen to thank you for your letter of 11th July about her meeting with the President of the Irish Republic.

Her Majesty has noted the content of your letter and I am to thank you for writing.

I am sorry to send you a disappointing reply but I am afraid we do not keep supplies of photographs of The Queen. I am therefore enclosing a list of photographic agencies from which you may buy a picture and return your postal order for five pounds.

Yours sincerely,

(KENNETH SCOTT)

Mr. J. Mackay.

PHOTOGRAPHS OF THE QUEEN AND THE ROYAL FAMILY
PHOTOGRAPHIC NEWS AGENCIES IN LONDON

Alpha Photo Press Agency,
63 Gee Street,
London, EC1V 3RS   071-253 7705/7803

Associated Press (Picture Library),
12, Norwich Street,
London, EC4A 1BT   071-353 1515
Ext:263

Barratt's Photo Press (Picture Desk),
68, Exmouth Market,
London EC1R 4RA   071-278 5661

The Hulton Picture Company
Unique House,   071-266 2662
21-31 Woodfield Road
London
W9 2BA   (includes
Keystone/Fox/Central/
Three Lions and Hulton picture
libraries)

Press Association Photos,
85 Fleet Street,
London EC4P 4BE   071-353 7440

Liam Mulvihill
Director General
Gaelic Athletic Association
Croke Park

Salem Court
Maxwell Road
Dublin 6

26 July 1993

Liam, a chara,

So some of the Dublin and Kildare players had a fisticuff fracas in the Croke Park tunnel yesterday. The way the media reacted, you would think a crime had been committed - a sportingly applied element of the physical force tradition has always been part of our national game. More to the point was Vinnie Murphy's disgraceful dismissal for a foul that left NOBODY injured. This refereeing trend towards penalising enthusiastic play will inevitably lead to soccer-style theatrics by prima donna pansies.

After the game some friends and I discussed the hostile media view of everything gaelic and, in particular, the satanic anti-Irish rantings of the Sunday Independent's self-styled cynic Danny Lynch. His recent venemous description of Saint Mother Teresa as "a tough old broad" bubbled predictably from his well-stirred cauldron of seething hatred of our proud national ethos. Some other random samples:

(1) He regularly refers to Gaelic Football and Hurling as "Bogball" and "Stick-Fighting" respectively;

(2) He hailed Down's famous All-Ireland victory as "The British representatives bringing the Sam Maguire back to the UK";

(3) He says Dublin defeats are extra humiliating because they are always inflicted by "Culchies or Bog Monsters" and that, while "other Counties also get beaten by woolybacks" it does not affect them as "their torsos are also of thick woollen texture".

Mr Mulvihill, I am considering initiating a public campaign to have this person's Irish citizenship removed. My thoughts include: seeking endorsements from top GAA stars, petitions at all major games, free adverts in match programmes, a catchy slogan like "Lynch Lackie Lynch"; all led by GAA people, NOT politicians - this is a NATIONAL issue. Do you think such a campaign would be useful?

Is mise le meas,

John Mackay

Mr John Mackay

PS I enclose a token donation to put towards the refurbishment of Croke Park, or to any legal actions needed against those who whinge at upgrading a GAELIC ground but flock to support SOCCER and RUGBY.

Cumann Lúthchleas Gael

Páirc an Chrócaigh, Áth Cliath 3
Guthán: 363222
Fax: 366420

ARD STIURTHOIR: LIAM Ó MAOLMHICHIL

6 August, 1993

Mr John Mackay

Salem Court,
Maxwell Road,
Dublin 6.

Dear Mr Mackay,

Thank you sincerely for your letter and enclosure. The Director General is currently away hence my communication. The person in question is Declan Lynch and I hope that you did not confuse him with me.

I can assure you that most people in the G.A.A. share your view. However, the general concensus is that any campaign of the nature suggested would only give the individual status and afford him notoriety, something which he obviously craves. Despite him and his ilk, the G.A.A. continues to Thrive. Attendances have increased by over fifty per cent and membership and organisation has improved significantly around the country. This is evident from new teams emerging regularly as serious contenders for major honours.

For the reasons stated we feel that he would be best ignored. Thank you for your sincere support.

Regards

Danny Lynch
P.R.O.

Salem Court
Maxwell Road
Dublin 6

25 May 1993

Michael D Higgins
Minister for Arts, Culture
and the Gaeltacht
Leinster House, Dublin 2

Dear Minister Higgins,

Your poetry reading on the Late Late Show inspired me to write the following two poems. The first is an upbeat and (hopefully!) humorous celebration of the rehabilitative impact of the Labour Party on the ethos of some in the pre-partnership Fianna Fail.

It is titled "<u>SINISTER MINISTER</u>":

> Sinister Minister Slippery Snake
> Sinister Minister On The Make
> Sinister Minister Overfed
> Here's Labour! The Sinister Minister's Dead!

There is, of course, a hidden irony: "Sinister" is Latin for "Left"! The second poem is a contemplative reflection, Durcanesque in treatment, on the paradoxical benefits of the proposed increase in Telecom charges.

It is titled "<u>YES THE PHONE COSTS MORE</u>":

> yes the phone costs more
> but only if you use it
> early in the day
> whereas if you choose to use it later instead
> it's cheaper
> by twopence
> every unit
> so the longer you talk
> the more you save
> and so the phone costs less
> instead

This is my first foray into poetry. What do you think? Are there any "how to" books or evening classes you would recommend? I believe I can also get tax-free status for being a poet - is this true? Please send me the details.

Again, congratulations on your recent promotion and your (literally!) inspirational fusion of the cultural and political spheres.

Yours sincerely,

John Mackay

John Mackay

OIFIG AN AIRE EALAÍON, CULTÚIR AGUS GAELTACHTA
OFFICE OF THE MINISTER FOR ARTS, CULTURE AND THE GAELTACHT

BAILE ÁTHA CLIATH 2
DUBLIN 2

16 June 1993

Mr John McKay,

Salem Court,
Maxwell Road,
Dublin 6.

Dear Mr Mckay,

Thank you for your letter of 24 May.   Thank you also for your
kind comments regarding my appointment as Minister.

I commend you on your initial efforts at writing poetry. I will
make enquiries regarding your queries about the assistance which
are available to poets. I will be in contact with you again as
soon as possible about this matter.

Yours sincerely,

MICHAEL D. HIGGINS T.D.,
MINISTER FOR ARTS, CULTURE
AND THE GAELTACHT

Salem Court
Maxwell Road
Dublin 6
Republic of Ireland

11 July 1993

President Bill Clinton
The White House
1,200 Pennsylvania Avenue
Washington D.C.
United States of America

Dear President Clinton,

The Comeback Kid has turned the corner! Your new spin doctor David
Gergen has certainly turned the opinion polls around, so let the sneerers
go dance on someone else's grave — preferably in Baghdad, where your
timely bombing of Saddam has let the world know that the trousers in the
White House are not worn by a big girl's blouse!

On St Patrick's Day when you teamed up with our Taoiseach Albert
Reynolds and two other Micks to harmonise "When Irish Eyes Are Smiling",
I quipped to my wife Dympna, "That barber's shop quartet must have used
a shilellagh for a tuning fork!" And, when you delayed Hair Force One
while Belgian crimper Cristophe fleeced you for $180, I retorted "It was
a snip at any price!" Mr President, the point is that I made inoffensive
jokes while the media Sweeney Todds scalped you.

When you first stepped forward as a candidate, with hair like Sam, the
bar-owner in Cheers — and a similar reputation as a ladies' man — I thought
it was an "only in America" joke. But when you were elected after showing
you had brains to match your looks, I thought, if young Bill Clinton can
make it from Little Rock to the White House, then surely an intellectual
with a responsible private life who is not promiscuous with money can
make it to the Aras in Ireland.

Mr Clinton, you have inspired me to run for the Presidency of Ireland
in 1997. As you know, we already have a fine incumbent but, like old George
Bush, President Robinson may not make a second term if she continues to
squander her energies on sweet F.A. (foreign affairs).

You successfully kept your campaign staff sharply focussed on the
overwhelmingly major national problem with a sign in your headquarters
wall that read: "The Economy, Stupid". I plan to do likewise but, in
Ireland, I fear that my sign will read "Everything, Stupid".

Naturally, it would be a breach of protocol for you to be seen to support
my campaign, but I would be deeply honoured if you could send me a signed
photograph of yourself as an inspirational wall-hanging in my campaign
headquarters. I enclose £5 to cover any expense.

Yours sincerely,

John Mackay

Mr John Mackay

Bill Clinton

Salem Court
Maxwell Road
Dublin 6

Mr Dermot Desmond,
National City Brokers,
Ferry House,
Lower Mount Street,
Dublin 2

2 March 1993

Dear Mr Desmond,

It is hardly a coincidence that Dr Michael Smurfit, Mr Chris Comerford, Mr Larry Goodman, Mr Charles Haughey and yourself are the subject of an eternal witch-hunt. But, as you have often said: "Profit is the booster that lifts the mediocre to magnificence". And your philosophy was always a challenge to the political pygmies and intellectual dwarves who are threatened by your enconomic enlightenment.

My good wife, Dympna, who shares our family secret that we benefited from the share price of one of your ventures, Emmetts Cream liquer, unfailingly toasts your business acumen with, "Give unto Caesar that which is Caesar's, but leave a little in the bottom of the glass for Dermo!"

Anyway, enough small talk. Dermot, there has been a disgusting conspiracy in our country, an evil web of begrudgery, filtering down from certain politicians, which threatens to destroy the enterprise culture so lovingly tended in our little garden in the far-flung geographic suburbs of north-western Europe.

I was always impressed that you never bothered with so-called "Third Level" education, preferring to learn the secret of life burrowing away at the coal-face of commerce. Michael Smurfit was never a man of letters either, but a master craftsman at collecting dollar bills.

Critics have excoriated Chris Comerford's no-nonsense approach to business and, though not always sweetness and light, he made the Sugar Company a rock on which to build the beacon of privatised industries. Then Charles Haughey, with Larry Goodman, showed that the farmer and the cowman should be friends, but neither had reckoned on the old biblical truism that a profit is never recognised in its own land.

Anyway, Dermot, don't get disheartened. There are still a few of us prepared to do what is right for the country — and the free-market liberal ideals for which we are prepared to fight. I enclose £5, a token donation to kick-start a fund to defend economic democracy. Please let me know what you want me to do and where you would wish me to do it.

Yours sincerely,

John Mackay

Mr John Mackay

DERMOT F. DESMOND

Mr John Mackay,

Salem Court,
Maxwell Road,
DUBLIN 6.

8th March, 1993.

Dear Mr Mackay,

Thank you for your kind letter and for the good wishes of your wife Dympna.

Let me assure you that I have a mental shield, which basically means that nobody will make me feel bad without my permission. If we are to develop in Ireland we must generate wealth in order to pay for the standards of health, education and social services we all want. The key objective for every Irish man and woman is to leave the place a little better for their children.

We must have high standards in business but we cannot hang people before the trial. We cannot take away other peoples good name in order that we may feel better, otherwise, we are working on the principal that the lowest common denominator shall succeed. We must adopt an approach whereby positive sentiment, action and risk-taking is encouraged and the reversal is admonished.

Finally, I appreciate your idea of a fund and your contribution, however, I am afraid that if I were to endorse this the Monopolies Commission or some other regulatory body would be on my back. I would like you to donate this to the Rape Crisis Centre in order that we all might get God's blessing in making Ireland a better place.

With kind regards,

Yours sincerely,

DERMOT F. DESMOND

encl.

Salem Court
Maxwell Road
Dublin 6

9 March 1993

Mons Jacques Delors
President
EC Commission
Brussels

Dear Mr Delors,

You've had it rough from the Little Englanders (Up yours, Delors, etc)
but the Irish and the French – nous sommes toujours amis, non? Oui! Vive
La France! Il ne faut pas parlez dans la salle de classe!

Here's the point. It has come to my attention in the Irish media that
the Republic of Ireland has been ear-marked for some IR£8 billion from
an expanded EC budget. Mons Delors, your generosity is only matched by
your vision and I would like to thank you personally for such altruistic
generosity.

However, while I personally admire and respect the Irish government,
frankly, my confidence in their economic acumen has never stretched to
giving them any more money than the minimum to keep out of prison for
not paying taxes.

I have calculated that my share of the IR£8 billion is somewhat around
IR£2,000. Can this be paid to me directly, cutting out the middle man,
so to speak? I am not joking. This is a serious request. I am a citizen
of Europe and you, as my President, are my servant (mon servant).

I enclose IR£5 to help with postage and administration. Please let me
know what arrangements you propose to make regarding direct payment as
your earliest convenience.

Yours sincerely,

John Mackay

Mr John Mackay

**COMMISSION
OF THE EUROPEAN
COMMUNITIES**

Office of the President

Brussels, 22 April 1993
CB/uod/3768

Dear Mr Mackay,

President Delors asked me to thank you for your letter of 9 March 1993.

I should point out that Community structural assistance is intended to improve infrastructure and other facilities in your country to speed up Ireland's process of catching-up the more prosperous countries of the Community. The money spent goes on useful projects approved by the Commission.

Unfortunately, your personal bank account is unlikely to qualify. I also am not joking. I therefore return your postal order for £5.

Nevertheless, the President appreciates your support.

Yours sincerely,

Chris BOYD

Mr Jon MACKAY

Salem Court
Maxwell Road
DUBLIN 6

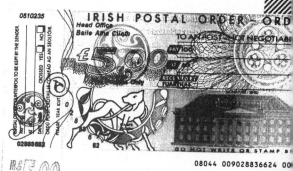

Rue de la Loi 200 – B-1049 Brussels – Belgium
Telephone: direct line 295.96.39 exchange 299.11.11 – Telex COMEU B 21877 – Telegraphic address COMEUR Brussels – Telefax 295.32.22

```
                                              Salem Court
                                              Maxwell Road
       The Commissioner                         Dublin 6
       Gardai Siochana
       Phoenix Park                           3 June 1993
       Dublin 8
```

Dear Commissioner Culligan,

I hope you can help me restore law and order in my house. Yesterday
my good wife Dympna was explaining the concepts of right and wrong to
our youngest, Suzie - a marvellous girl, but prone to such unhelpful
tendencies as unneccessarily independent thinking.

Suzie was proclaiming the merits of so-called "criminal's rights",
which Dympna and I agree should extend no further than the right to be
securely locked up in a cell, but a concept which one of Suzie's "liberal"
teachers seems to extend into all sorts of other areas.

Just as Dympna was gaining the upper hand, an RTE advert for Telecom's
"phone watch" intervened. This "advert" started with the words: "The
Irish Burglars Association wishes you were here..." followed by some
foreign holiday type music. "There!" exclaimed Suzie triumphantly, "If
they have an Association, they clearly have rights".

Dympna was flummoxed, and not a little angry. Surely an Association
of CRIMINALS should be illegal? Surely it is ENTIRELY IRRESPONSIBLE for
a semi-state body that is PAID FOR BY OUR TAXES to be promoting their
existence? Dympna and I have been robbed THREE TIMES, probably by an
elected officer of the IBA who is even now chuckling away at the publicity
his insane group is receiving.

Suzie has since become intolerable, reciting the advert over and over
and openly laughing at her mother, though not in my presence. Commissioner
Culligan, I would appreciate your advice - should we ignore her, try to
reason with her, or lock her in her room? Do you have any guidelines for
humane but effective domestic incarceration? And what can we do about
getting the offending "advert" off the national airwaves?

Yours sincerely,

John Mackay

Mr John Mackay

PS I think I'll also write to Telecom Eireann about this.

PPS I enclose a token contribution to the fight against lawlessness.
Put it to good use!

AN GARDA SIOCHANA

Any reply to this communication should be
addressed to:

  Commissioner,
    Garda Síochána,
    Phoenix Park,
    Dublin 8.

and the following number quoted:

OIFIG AN CHOIMISINEARA,

BAILE ÁTHA CLIATH.

10th June 1993

Mr. John Mackay,

Salem Court,
Maxwell Road,
Dublin 6.

Dear Mr. Mackay,

I am directed by the Commissioner to refer to your letter of 3rd
June 1993.

At the outset, I must congratulate you on rearing a perfectly
normal modern young daughter, Suzie, who, to judge from your
letter, will certainly keep you on your toes.

In relation to the Telecom advertisement, the "Irish Burglars
Association" and its "spokesman" on holiday is a theatrical
invention of the advertisers in order to convey to the viewer
that criminals gain very considerably because house owners do not
always secure their property. In this case they are suggesting a
particular security product. If you have a complaint to make
regarding the contents of the advertisement you should contact
R.T.E. and/or the Advertising Standards Authority For Ireland,
IPC House, Shelbourne Road, Dublin 4.

You enclosed a postal order for £5 with your letter. As a
taxpayer you are already contributing to public crime prevention
and policing operations. I am enclosing your postal order and
thank you very much for your thoughtfulness.

Yours sincerely,

John V. Kennedy

JOHN V. KENNEDY
SUPERINTENDENT
PRIVATE SECRETARY
TO COMMISSIONER

TELECOM PhoneWatch

A **NYNEX** | TELECOM EIREANN Company

Unit 4, Sandyford Park
Burton Hall Road
Sandyford Industrial
Estate
Sandyford
Co. Dublin
Telephone: (01) 2956900
Fax: (01) 2958199
International Telephone:
+353-1-2956900

16th June 1993

Mr John Mackay

Salem Court
Maxwell Road
Dublin 6

Dear Mr Mackay

Thank you for your letter of June 3rd to the Chief Executive of Telecom Eireann
Mr Fergus McGovern, in relation to the Telecom PhoneWatch "Irish Burglar's Association"
advertisement. Mr McGovern has passed the letter to me for my attention.

Before going ahead with the advertisement, we tested it on a representative sample of the
public, especially as one of our concerns was that the "Irish Burlar's Association" be
recognised and understood by the public as purely fictitious. No reservations were raised
in relation to this point during the tests, nor have we received any other complaints in
relation to the advertisement since the campaign began. I might add that the advertisement
had to adhere to RTE's advertising code before it could be broadcast and to the advertising
code of the national newspapers before it could be printed.

We are satisfied that the advertisement does not breach any of the recognised advertising
standards currently in place. However, as a parent I can fully understand your concern that
your daughter recognise the difference between right and wrong. That said, the root of the
problem would appear to be the concept of "criminal rights" put forward by the "liberal"
school teacher you mentioned.

As requested, I have enclosed a brochure on our security system. Thank you once again for
your letter which I trust I have answered to your satisfaction.

Yours sincerely

Nick Quigley
General Manager

Directors: J. P. Joyce (Chairman), G. W. Kassebaum (USA), J. Kaufman (USA), D. McManus (USA), M. J. Sheridan
Registered Office: Telecom PhoneWatch Ltd., Merrion House, Merrion Road, Dublin 4.   Registered in Ireland No: 162566.

Salem Court
Maxwell Road
Dublin 6

23 Feb 1993

Bishop Casey
c/o Bishop's Palace,
Galway

Dear Bishop Casey,

I write for advice. I well understand your "situation" as I have a cousin in the priesthood who, like your good self, has betrayed his marriage to Christ. He has also, somewhat like your good self, fathered two beautiful baby twins out of secular wedlock.

I myself am happily married, with a faithful wife, Dympna, and a teenage son and daughter - but happily here at home we do not face the same magnitude of university fees as you do in Connecticut.

Indeed, your problems coincide with my cousin's in more ways than one, for his "mistress" is now demanding Church money for the twins' upkeep in light of the revelations of the money you paid to Ms Murphy.

My cousin, not being a Bishop, has no access to Diocesan accounts, and he does not believe his particular Bishop would interpret the scope of such funds as humanely as you did.

I can personally afford to meet the requested paternity payments by deleting from the family budget our regular contributions to the Church. My cousin is grateful for this, but his mistress insists that the Church, and not I, should pay the money.

I have explained to her that I am just paying directly what would have been an indirect payment had we made our Church contributions in Galway. She seems satisfied with this explanation, though now my wife is worried that "people will talk" if we stop contributing to the Church. What advice would you have?

Yours sincerely,

John Mackay

Mr John Mackay

Salem Court
Maxwell Road
Dublin 6

Charles J Haughey
Kinsaley
County Dublin

17 Feb 1993

Dear Mr Haughey,

I am writing to you as a citizen of Ireland about a matter of vital national importance. As our very currency stumbles through multiple self-inflicted political minefields, it is becoming increasingly clear that you should never have vacated the Taoiseachship. Does anyone seriously believe that you would have fudged and fecked around like the current cabinet of economic incompetents and political amateurs?

After some years abroad, I have recently returned to my native land and I now plead with you, Mr Haughey, to reconsider your too-hasty retirement. "Consensus" Reynoldsite politics may seem superficially "reasonable" but, as you and I well know, progress depends on the unreasonable man. Ask Alan (where is he now?) Dukes!

And yes, of course, you were opposed by an inconsequential rabble of small, petty people, obsessed with insignificant so-called "scandals" of a decade ago, and burning inside with jealousy of your political wisdom and courage, your proud Irish republicanism, your patronage of the arts and the bishops, your sense of your place in history – your very political essence, Mr Haughey, to which they could not aspire and so conspired to destroy, scrambling feverishly to add their fingerprints to the dagger that was Doherty's.

You, Mr Haughey, were not merely a political Houdini but a modern European Cuchulainn, unfazed by "scandals" that would have ended the career of a mere political mortal. You, and only you, could have left Fianna Fail as strong as it was when you left. You owe it to yourself and the nation to return to active politics, biding your time with dignity until your invisible successor is seen for the visionless pet-food-manufacturer that he is.

I and some colleagues are currently planning to launch a non-party-political "Bring Back Charles J Haughey" campaign. We have a sizable nest-egg available, and we do not seek any "seed capital" from you. Do we need your formal endorsement, or should that come after the launch? We bow to your wisdom in this area. At least, please let us know that you have not definitively closed the door to the historic return to power that is inevitable once people realise that you in fact stemmed, not caused, the recent and ongoing drop in Fianna Fail fortunes.

Yours sincerely,

John Mackay

Mr John Mackay

PS I believe you knew my father – JJ Mackay – in the sixties.

Abbeville

KINSALEY COUNTY DUBLIN

Mr. John Mackay,   2nd March 1993.

Salem Court,
Maxwell Road,
Dublin 6.

Dear John,

Thank you very much for your interesting letter of the 17th February.

I think it would be helpful if we were to meet and discuss your suggestion.   If you agree, perhaps you would contact Marie Sheahan at 8453927 to arrange something mutually convenient.

I greatly appreciate the kind sentiments you have expressed and look forward to talking to you.

With kindest regards,

Yours sincerely,

Salem Court
Maxwell Road
Dublin 6

25 May 1993

Mr Peter Shanley
Chairman, Bar Council
Four Courts
Dublin 7

Dear Mr Shanley,

I am soliciting your help in a quest which concerns our only son, Tobias now 22. He has a lowly though respectable arts degree from UCD but, instead of settling for the civil service or something sensible, he has his heart set on becoming a barrister. Mr Shanley, although he has high hopes, realistically, it could prove tricky.

Toby will brook no dilution of his ambition which, frankly, was fired up by the publicity concerning barristers and judges and the Shelbourne hotel. My wife Dympna and I have heard him in his bedroom pretending to be a barrister into the mirror on the wardrobe. We think he is very good and Dympna bought him a gavel in a city auction room recently which he uses frequently to rule on domestic tiffs.

It may well be that our son was never destined to be attorney general, or a judge, or even become one of the leading counsel in the State: we don't have money or position in society and therefore don't expect to eat at the officers' table. But you work in the courts and must know that for every gifted Mr Shanley there are dozens of drones picking up six figure annual incomes for just turning up in a wig and gown.

Toby was always something of a show-off, riding his bicycle with no hands and that sort of thing, which, while a tiresome trait in, say, a quantity surveyor, must be a bonus in your trade. I'm sure you agree.

Lets get into a huddle: we understand it is possible to study for the Bar at the King's Inns, and you, Sir, are particularly well placed to assist our eldest boy become Tobias Mackay BL.

If you could use your influence, "pull" or whatever it is called in drawing room society, to have him accepted as a student at the King's Inns, the Mackay family will serve you and yours as indentured servants, if that is what is required.

Presumably barristers, like the rest of us, can always use a few pounds, and I enclose £5 as an initial down-payment for any "expenses" you may incur interceding for our Toby with such meddlesome parkers at the King's Inns as may question his educational qualifications.

Yours sincerely,

John Mackay

Mr John Mackay

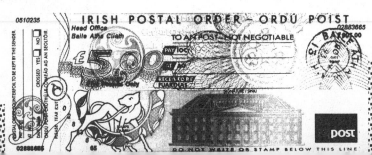

THE BAR COUNCIL

P.O. Box 2424, Law Library, Four Courts, Dublin 7 Tel: 8735689 / 8735535 Fax: 8735624

Mr. John Mackay,

Salem Court,
Maxwell Road,
Dublin 6.

25 June 1993

Dear Sir,

I have been asked by the Chairman of the Bar Council, Peter Shanley SC, to reply to your letter of 25 May 1993. I am returning your letter and postal order in the sum of £5.00.

The admission of students to King's Inns is a matter entirely for the authorities at the Inns and one in which the Bar Council plays no role.

The Chairman does not propose to enter into any correspondence on this matter.

Yours faithfully,

John Dowling
Director

THE COUNCIL OF THE BAR OF IRELAND

Ivan Yates TD
Finance Spokesperson
Fine Gael
leinster House
Dublin 2

Salem Court
Maxwell Road
Dublin 6

11 June 1993

Dear Mr Yates,

My family live in Wexford, where you always get their number one, as indeed you did mine before my move to the big smoke some time back.

As a bookie, you're clearly aware of the old gaming insurance of the "each way bet", and you certainly covered all the options on the tax amnesty issue: Go to jail, go directly to jail, do not pass go, do not collect the 90% tax write-off I proposed last week!

Your pragmatic adaptability exceeds that of many a slippery Minister twice your age, and augurs well for your future Taoiseachship. Well done - I enclose a token donation to your next election campaign.

Here's another plan, Ivan; not strictly your remit, but you've got the style to both float it and shoot it down yourself if need be.

What about an OVERALL crime amnesty? Release ALL prisoners who have served more than 10% of their sentences. Throw out 90% of ALL criminal cases pending before the courts.

Result? A fresh start for everyone, more money for the exchequer, and room in the jails for future offenders - including tax evaders who ignore the current tax amnesty!

Perhaps you could run it past the escape committee, see how far down the tunnel it digs itself, and hurl it back into the dungeons if Johhny Bruton kicks up a fuss. What do you think?

Yours sincerely,

John Mackay

Mr John Mackay

16th June, 1993.

Mr. John Mackay,

Salem Court,
Maxwell Road,
Dublin 6.

Dear John,

I thank you for your most informative and interesting letter, which I enjoyed reading.

I have forwarded your very generous subscription to the Enniscorthy town Branch account of the Fine Gael Party.

I note your proposal in relation to a crime amnesty and I suppose it is as convincing an argument as you can get against the tax amnesty by way of analogy. When the debate comes before the Dail, I hope to use it to good effect.

I thank you for your very kind comments.

Please convey my very best wishes to all your family in Wexford. I hope that you are enjoying the high life in the big city.

Many thanks again and best wishes,

Yours sincerely

IVAN YATES, T.D.

P.S. I return your S.A.E. as one of the few perks of T.D.'s is to have free postage.

                                                                Salem Court
                                                                Maxwell Road
                                                                   Dublin 6

Albert Reynolds
Taoiseach   2 Mar 1993
Leinster House
Dublin 2

Dear Taoiseach,

    Many thanks indeed for your prompt, courteous and personal response
to my recent letter. It is heartening that your heavy schedule as Head
of Our State and a player on the World Stage has not prevented your
hands-on "man-of-the-people" personality from permeating your business
correspondence. May I in future letters refer to you as Albert?
    Many thanks also for your promise to enquire with the IDA about the
possibility of manufacturing Irish-made dogfood bowls modelled as
plexiglass dinner plates. I have taken the liberty of writing myself to
the IDA, enclosing some outline potential design drafts drawn up by my
wife Dympna (she is not by any standards a professional graphic designer,
but she has done a FAS course in art and has access to an Apple Macintosh
computer for technical drawing). I must also stress that neither I nor
Dympna would insist on excessive personal remuneration, beyond standard
royalties, for providing these ideas - we must all contribute to the
shared task of national economic recovery.
    I was sorry - but not surprised - to see the visionless media cynically
blame your good self for the Digital company pulling out of Galway when
we live on a global world-wide planet. I would argue that: "the Digital
job-glass is as much one third full as two thirds empty" (feel free to
use this as a perspective-shifting quote, without attribution, when
commenting further on the issue).
    Anyway, thanks again for your prompt attention to what I am sure is
a very small matter on your agenda. You can rest assured that I will be
contacting your Mr Farrell about contributing to the Party.

    Yours sincerely,

    John Mackay

    Mr John Mackay

    PS I am also considering becoming actively involved in the Fianna Fail
Party. I cannot do so yet, but I will soon be moving abode to either Cork
or Galway, and will at that stage have spare time on my hands. Who would
be the appropriate "contact person" in these areas?

Oifig an Taoisigh
Office of the Taoiseach

Ref. No. FO/35.

5 March, 1993.

Mr. John Mackay,

Salem Court,
Maxwell Road,
Dublin 6.

Dear John,

The Taoiseach, Mr. Albert Reynolds, T.D., has asked me to write to you in response to your recent letter addressed to him.

The Taoiseach recommends that when you move house to either Cork or Galway you should then contact him indicating your new address as he will then be in a position to make arrangements for the local Fianna Fail organisation to contact you.

The Taoiseach hopes this clarifies matters for you.

Yours sincerely

Private Secretary.

Oifig an Taoisigh, Tithe an Rialtais, Baile Átha Cliath 2.
Office of the Taoiseach, Government Buildings, Dublin 2.

Salem Court
Maxwell Road
Dublin 6

2 Mar 1993

Kiaran McGowan,
Managing Director,
IDA,
Wilton Park House,
Wilton Place,
Dublin 2

Dear Mr McGowan,

No doubt you have by now received a letter from the Taoiseach about the potential commercial viability of manufacturing Irish-made dogfood bowls modelled as plexiglass dinner plates. As the enclosed letter shows, the enquiry is on foot of a suggestion of mine.

I write to assure you that, despite the courteous first-name-terms tone with which Albert and I correspond, I would wish the enquiry to be treated strictly on its commercial merits and not be influenced by other considerations.

The concept is domestically inspired - as with so many inventions - in that my daughter's spaniel puppy will not eat his dinner unless we feed him on a family plate. However, none of the petshops I have checked with stock dogfood bowls modelled as dinner plates. Hence the idea. Hence the enquiry. Bounce it around and see if it breaks.

I enclose for your perusal some outline potential design drafts drawn up by my wife Dympna. Perhaps you could send them "down the line" as possible prototypes to whichever of your people has been assigned this project.

I must stress that I wish this enquiry to be treated strictly on its commercial merits. If it is a non-starter, please say so. If it runs, or even splutters, send it along to an appropriate entrepreneur.

Yours sincerely,

John Mackay

John Mackay

PS I must stress that neither I nor Dympna would insist on excessive personal remuneration, beyond standard royalties, for these ideas - we must all contribute to the shared task of national recovery.

PPS The IDA has of late come in for carping criticism from the political pygmies and layabouts around Leinster House - ignore them, get stuck in there, you are doing your job, and doing it well.

PROPOSED DRAFT DESIGN FOR
IRISH-MANUFACTURED
DOGFOOD BOWLS MODELLED AS
PLEXIGLASS DINNER PLATES

Salem Court
Maxwell Road
Dublin 6

2 Mar 1993

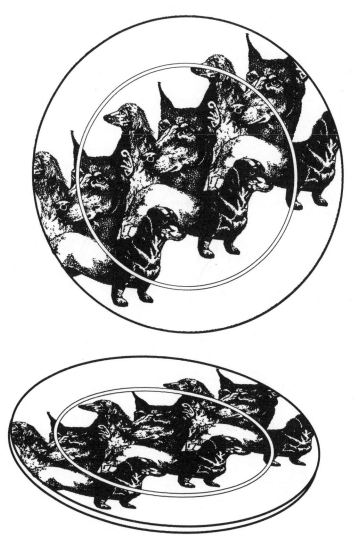

SUBMITTED TO MR KIARAN McGOWAN, MANAGING DIRECTOR, IDA,
FOR USE IN COMMERCIAL VIABILITY ENQUIRY
INSTIGATED BY AN TAOISEACH, MR ALBERT REYNOLDS TD

INDUSTRIAL DEVELOPMENT
AUTHORITY OF IRELAND

IDA
IRELAND

WILTON PARK HOUSE
WILTON PLACE
DUBLIN 2   IRELAND
TELEPHONE (01) 686633
FACSIMILE (01) 603703

KIERAN McGOWAN
MANAGING DIRECTOR
CHAIRMAN OF EXECUTIVE BOARD

Mr John Mackay

Salem Court
Maxwell Road
Dublin 6

5 March 1993

Dear Mr Mackay

On behalf of the Managing Director, Mr Kieran McGowan, I would like to acknowledge receipt of your letter dated 2 March 1993 regarding your proposal for the manufacture of dog bowls.

Mr McGowan is away from the office at present but I will bring your letter to his attention on his return.

Yours sincerely

Edel Finan
Managing Director's Office

IDA IRELAND

INDUSTRIAL DEVELOPMENT
AUTHORITY OF IRELAND

WILTON PARK HOUSE
WILTON PLACE
DUBLIN 2   IRELAND
TELEPHONE (01) 686633
FACSIMILE (01) 603703

KIERAN McGOWAN
MANAGING DIRECTOR
CHAIRMAN OF EXECUTIVE BOARD

Mr John Mackay

Salem Court
Maxwell Road
Dublin 6

11 March 1993

Dear Mr Mackay

Thank you for your letter of 2 March 1993 in relation to the potential commercial viability of manufacturing Irish-made dogfood bowls modelled as plexiglass dinner plates.

From your letter it appears that you do not wish to manufacture the product yourself.   Therefore, perhaps the best way to progress your idea would be to talk to existing manufacturers or companies with marketing capability to sell the product nationally or internationally who would then have your product manufactured on a sub-contract basis.

I have asked Mr Colm Mac Fhionnlaoich from our Small Business Division to make contact with you to discuss your proposal and introduction to potential manufacturers.

Yours sincerely

Salem Court
Maxwell Road
Dublin 6

Ms Niamh Breathnach
Minister for Education   25 May 1993
Department of Education
Marlborough Street
Dublin 1

Dear Ms Breathnach,

Conratulations on ignoring the begrudgers and bringing your daughter
into power with you as your secretary. You have nothing to be ashamed
of, and neither has Mr Stagg - The Family is the sacred rock upon which
our Constitution is built, and you seem the sort of person who is prepared
to look after your own.

My wife Dympna tells me that you were attacked by your Labour Party
colleagues for speaking at your first Party meeting! Is this true? If
so, you certainly have the last laugh on them now. As Education Minister
you control the destiny of our children, and if your talent and compassion
are recognised you may well be our first woman Tanaiste.

Ms Breathneach, my own daughter, Susie, is finishing school this year
- a bright and perceptive girl, with modern socialist leanings. Like your
own daughter, she would really love to work in the Dail - important work
colleagues, long holidays and a chance to serve her community. What would
be the chance of you whispering a few words into the relevant ears? I
can send a CV if you like.

You, of course, realise that my motivation is entirely honourable but,
to avoid any media cynicism, I will of course keep the matter under my
hat if you succeed.

Yours sincerely,

John Mackay

Mr John Mackay

PS I enclose a token donation to your next election campaign fund. I
must stress that this is of course TOTALLY UNCONNECTED with your success
or otherwise in sorting out Susie - fiscal integrity is no less important
than familial solidarity.

Oifig an Aire Oideachais
Sráid Maoilbhríde
Baile Átha Cliath 1

Telefón 734700
Facs   729093

Office of the Minister for Education
Marlborough Street
Dublin 1

Telephone 734700
Fax   729093

Mr. John Mackay,

Maxwell Road,
Dublin 6.

Constituency Office
Phone: 6717187/6717010

Dear Mr. Mackay,

I would like to say a sincere thank you for the kind words of
encouragement expressed in your recent correspondence – letters
such as yours are an exception to the rule in my line of work.

Please do not misunderstand my motive in returning your donation
to my campaign funds –it has never been my policy to accept
private contributions – but I would like to thank you for the
thought.

With regard to your wish to obtain employment for your daughter,
I will certainly keep Susie's name in mind should I hear of any
vacancies in the Oireachtas.

If agreeable, may I suggest that you contact your local Labour
Party representative, Pat Upton, who would also assist you in the
matter.

Perhaps you could forward her Curriculum Vitae to either Pat or
myself.

Once again, thank you for your kindness – it is much appreciated.

Yours sincerely,

NIAMH BHREATHNACH T.D.,
MINISTER FOR EDUCATION.

3/ May, 1993.

The Managing Director,
Galtee Food Products,
Pork Processors,
19 Parkmore Industrial Estate,
Dublin 12

Salem Court
Maxwell Road
Dublin 6

9 March 1993

Copy to the Advertising Standards Association

Dear sir,

Firstly, congratulations on a magnificent product line – my breakfast would not be the same without the satisfying sizzle of Galtee. However, I am frankly shocked by your current radio advert, which starts with the line "Back in the way back when, when the Bay City Rollers were musically challenged, a pound of Galtee rashers cost less than a pound..". Well! Why this offensive and entirely gratuitous insult to one of Scotland's most popular music combos and unrivalled cultural icons of their generation? I presume you think that sanctioning this peurile and racist "humour" is somehow funny? And please, sir, do not seek to pass the blame "down the line" – you are the man at the top who grinds the monkey's organ.

Sir, when you insult the Bay City Rollers, you insult the entire Scottish nation. Even today, my son Toby's bedroom is – unchanged from the seventies – a very shrine to the tartan "rockin' Rollers". What group today could match the perfect harmonies and emotive intensity of such timeless classics as "Bye Bye Baby Baby Bye Bye"? Many are the musical fields graced by Irish greats, but only in the shape of the indomitable U2 have we come close to the global adulation enjoyed by the Bay City Rollers.

I must ask you, sir, to explain this uncalled for lapse in Galtee taste, and to remove the offending advert herewith from the national airwaves. It is with regret that I write this letter, and send a copy to the Advertising Standards Association.

I must stress that this complaint should not be interpreted as reflecting on your rashers, which are of excellent quality and value and are done an unwarranted disservice by this crass and racist offensiveness to the musical culture and heritage of a neighbourly nation.

Yours faithfully,

John Mackay

Mr John Mackay

**DAIRYGOLD
FOOD PRODUCTS**

Cahir Hill, Mitchelstown, Co. Cork, Ireland. Tel: 025-24300. Fax: 025-84322.

18th March, 1993.

Mr. John Mackay.

Salem Court,
Maxwell Road,
Dublin 6.

Dear Mr. Mackay,

Thank you for your recent letter regarding our current radio advertisement for Galtee Traditional Gold Sausages and your kind comments with regard to the Galtee product range.

I was disappointed to learn of the deep offence, you and your family have recently experienced by our new radio campaign for Galtee Traditional Gold Sausages and especially with our reference to the Bay City Rollers.

It was never our intention to cause crass and racist offensiveness to the musical culture and heritage of a neighbourly nation but to associate the popularity of the group to our product.

It was for the groups popularity and huge appeal to today's young housewife, that the Bay City Rollers were specifically chosen. The campaign was designed to remind today's housewife of the quality times they experienced in their youth and to associate these times to a quality product, Galtee Traditional Gold Sausages. I believe that although bands may come and go, the appeal of the Bay City Rollers, 15 years on, is still unchallenged especially in the eyes of their fans. Today, we in Galtee proudly associate our product to the Bay City Rollers and our campaign was intended to compliment rather than insult the band.

On behalf of Galtee Food Products, I would like to apologise for any offence caused, but for the forementioned reasons, I am unable to withdraw the campaign at the present time.

Yours sincerely,
GALTEE FOOD PRODUCTS.

JOHN O'SULLIVAN.
GENERAL MANAGER.

Galtee Food Products Society Limited.
Registered Office: Fermoy Road, Mitchelstown, Co. Cork, Ireland. Reg. No: 4381R
A Subsidiary of Dairygold Co-Operative Society Limited.

ADVERTISING STANDARDS
AUTHORITY FOR IRELAND

IPC HOUSE,
35/39 SHELBOURNE RD.,
DUBLIN 4.
TELEPHONE (01)-608766
FAX (01)-608113

In reply please quote
Our Ref: RT/933/7.am

15th March 1993

Mr John Mackay,

Salem Court,
Maxwell Road,
Dublin 6.

Dear Mr Mackay,

We received your recent letter about the radio commercial for Galtee rasher.

As you may know the function of the Advertising Standards Authority for Ireland is to ensure that advertisers comply with the requirements of the Code of Advertising Standards.

In the case of RTE, all commercials must comply also with the RTE Code of Standards for Broadcast Advertising and are subject to prior clearance by the RTE Copy Clearance Committee. Accordingly, complaints concerning television or radio commercials are conveyed to RTE for their consideration in the first instance.

We have therefore advised RTE of your complaint and you may expect to receive a direct reply from them in the matter in the near future.

Yours sincerely,

Noel McMahon,
CHIEF EXECUTIVE.

Chairman:
Dr. Joseph C. McGough, K.M.
Chief Executive and Secretary
Noel McMahon
Registered in Dublin No. 8221

Dublin 4, Ireland   Baile Átha Cliath 4, Éire   Radio Telefís Éireann
Telephone 01 643111   Telefón 01 643111
Telefax 01 643080   Telefax 01 643080
Telex 93700   Teleics 93700
Direct Line 01 64   Líne Díreach 01 64

23rd March 1993

Mr. John Mackay

Salem Court
Maxwell Road
Dublin 6

Dear Mr. Mackay,

Mr. Noel McMahon of the Advertising Standards Authority
for Ireland has passed me a copy of your letter of 9th
March regarding a radio advertisement for Galtee Rashers.

Following your complaint we have listened again to this
commercial but we do not believe that the reference to
the Bay City Rollers should be taken as a serious comment
on the musical ability of this band. Rather we see it as
a fun comment reflecting the fact that, while the Bay
City Rollers are a hugely successful band, they are not
to everybody's liking and the 'Galtee Rasher Man' is
obviously of this minority group. I am afraid we cannot
accept that the reference to the Bay City Rollers would
cause offence to listeners. Under the circumstances we
would not be in a position to ask for any amendment to
this advertisement.

Yours sincerely,

Brian Pierce
Manager Radio Sales

Salem Court
Maxwell Road
Dublin 6

David Begg
General Secretary   23 Feb 1993
Communications Workers Union
North Circular Road

Dear Mr Begg,

Postmen of the world unite! My father was a postman, and I delivered
leaflets in college before being forced to leave Ireland for work.

Having recently returned to Dublin, I am amusingly told that you broke
your own strike last year to deliver circulars from yourselves supporting
the strike and opposing strike breaking! Nothing wrong with such a
superficial contradiction - strategic flexibility is what counts in such
circumstances.

As you so rightly argued, your members wanted to work but management
wouldn't let them. Management may simplistically counter that the new
part-time workers wanted to work but you wouldn't let them, but you and
I both know that this is just a cynical cloak for savage casualisation
of the workforce.

It is outrageous for management to insist that they can stop paying
a part-time employee, simply because the work that he was employed to
do has finished. It is like arguing that I can stop paying my plumber,
simply because he has finished fixing the leak. A job is a job is a job
and it doesn't end simply because there is no work to do.

Anyway, here's the point of my letter. Irish trade unions must
resolutely stand up to management's savage intransigence before the
current Spring/ Reynolds/ Thatcherite government is allowed to revive
the horrors of smashing the unions Scargill-style. True grit, and more
of it needed. The barricades must stay standing.

I would like to do what I can to help ensure you can stay in the vanguard
of protecting Irish workers. I enclose a token donation - not much, I
know, but I'm not a "fat cat". Also, what arrangements should I make to
contribute regularly to the union for future strikes?

     Yours sincerely,

     John Mackay

     Mr John Mackay

PS a colleague of my father's in the early years of the Free State had
a question raised in the first Dail challenging the purchase by the State
of London-made brass buttons for postmen's uniforms. I presume that this
scandal has ended - perhaps you could confirm?

COMMUNICATIONS WORKERS' UNION
CEARD CHUMANN OIBRITHE CUMARSÁIDE

575 NORTH CIRCULAR ROAD, DUBLIN 1
TELEPHONE 366388   FAX 365582

26 February 1993

Mr. John MacKay

Salem Court
Maxwell Road
Dublin 6

Dear Mr. McKay,

I am writing to acknowledge with thanks receipt of your letter and enclosure of 23rd instant.

Your contribution is most welcome and I will ensure that it is put into the union's contingency fund, which was indeed seriously depleted during the dispute. It has however, come back up to its normal level now. If we do become involved in any further disputes of course additional contributions would be most welcome at that time. At the same time, I hope that this will not be necessary because, I am sure you will appreciate, most workers live from hand to mouth and suffer a great deal of hardship when on strike.

With regard to your enquiry concerning the brass buttons for the postman's uniform the position has changed substantially. The company no longer use these buttons and indeed the traditional uniform is gone as well. Some years ago, they got Paul Costello, the fashion designer to create a new uniform and this is manufactured in Ireland.

Thank you once again for your interest.

Yours sincerely,

David T. Begg
GENERAL SECRETARY

Salem Court
Maxwell Road
Dublin 6
Republic of Ireland

11 July 1993

Mrs Hillary Rodham-Clinton
First Lady
The White House
1,200 Pennsylvania Avenue
Washington D.C.
United States of America

Dear Mrs Rodham Clinton,

Shame on the misogynists branding you a harridan for introducing the nose-gay of feminism to a US government reeking of old socks and testosterone. Take heart: it is less of a cross to carry bossy boots jibes than the slings and arrows of dumb blonde jokes. And your burden is an inspiration for women who aspire to the key of the executive lavatory. Everybody's First lady should be a Mrs Rodham Clinton.

I'm hoping my wife, Dympna, will use you as a role model to assist me on the nursery slopes of my ambition and be my sherpa to the summit of my political Everest: John MacKay wants to be President of Ireland in 1997, allowing the incumbent, Mrs Robinson, to take a welcome break from her public duties to catch up on her domestic responsibilities.

Already Dympna is putting together a womens election group to help me woo the feminist vote and a group of my football buddies have organised a masculist group to reassure Irish men that they have nothing to fear from the fairer sex but fear of the fairer sex itself!

We want to reproduce the team image projected by your good self and your husband. Just as you are known collectively to the political pundits as "Billary Clinton", we hope to be labelled in Ireland as "Johnpna Mackay". Dympna may also challenge Mrs Robinson to a culinary cookie recipe contest, just as you so successfully did with old Barbie Bush. What do you think? Like Ross Perot, we're all ears.

Naturally, we realise that it would be a breach of protocol for you to be seen to support our campaign, but I would greatly appreciate if you could send us the winning recipe from your campaign cookie contest. I enclose £5 to cover the cost of same.

Yours sincerely,

John Mackay

Mr John Mackay

PS Incidentally, I love your new haircut. Did the Belgian crimper Cristophe do the coiffing?

PPS Regards to Chelsea, Socks and Mr P.

THE WHITE HOUSE
WASHINGTON

July 23, 1993

Mr. John Mackay
Salem House, Maxwell Road
Dublin 6
Ireland,

Dear Mr. Mackay:

Thank you very much for your thoughtful and entertaining letter to Mrs. Clinton. We greatly appreciate your words of support and encouragement.

I am delighted to send you a copy of Mrs. Clinton's cookie recipe. Because we can not accept money for postage, your check is enclosed.

Thank you again for writing.

Sincerely yours,

Alice J. Pushkar
Director of Correspondence
for the First Lady

THE WHITE HOUSE

Hillary Clinton's Chocolate Chip Cookies

1 1/2 cups unsifted all-purpose flour
1 teaspoon salt
1 teaspoon baking soda
1 cup solid vegetable shortening
1 cup firmly packed light brown sugar
1/2 cup granulated sugar
1 teaspoon vanilla
2 eggs
2 cups old-fashioned rolled oats
1 (12-ounce) package semi-sweet chocolate chips

Preheat oven to 350 degrees. Grease baking sheets. Combine flour, salt and baking soda. Beat together shortening, sugars and vanilla in a large bowl until creamy. Add eggs, beating until light and fluffy. Gradually beat in flour mixture and rolled oats. Stir in chocolate chips. Drop batter by well-rounded teaspoonsful on to greased baking sheets. Bake 8 to 10 minutes or until golden. Cool cookies on sheets on wire rack for 2 minutes. Remove cookies to wire rack to cool completely.

Hillary Rodham Clinton

IRISH
Head Office
Balle Átha Cliath

0510235

£5

                                                        Salem Court
                                                        Maxwell Road
Mr Joe Barry   Dublin 6
Director General
RTE   25 May 1993
Donnybrook
Dublin 4

    Dear Mr Barry,

    On a recent holiday in California my wife Dympna and I took a three
hour, thirty dollar trip in a luxury coach choc-a-block with star-struck
rubberneckers following a pre-planned route around the Hollywood homes
of the rich and famous. At the end of the Stars' Homes Tour, I remembered
Mr Gay Byrne's regular pleas for potential entrepreneurs to bring home
good ideas, and said to Dympna, "this is money for old rope, let's do the
same when we get home and cut RTE in on the action."
    Here's the plan: StarTour Eireann Ltd. I've begun negotiations with
Bus Eireann for a suitable coach, so don't concern yourself with that.
Your contribution would be the inside track: for instance fees earned
and other "confidential" information like amusing anecdotes about rows
in the studios and personality clashes. By way of example, we heard on
the Hollywood tour that Rock Hudson was something of a big girl's blouse
and that the late J. Edgar Hoover shared both a bed and a tailor with
Marilyn Monroe!
    Mr Barry, I would appreciate it if you could send personal details,
including home adresses of: the cast of Glenroe, Mr RTE himself, Dr Gay
Byrne, Mr Pat Kenny, Ms Fionnuala Sweeney, Mr Gerry Ryan, Ms Bibi Baskin,
Mr Joe Duffy, Ms Marion Finucane, Mr Charlie Bird, Mr Charles Mitchell,
Mr Mike Murphy, Mr Bill O'Herlihy and Mr Jimmy Magee.
    At least two of the stars would be expected to provide light
refreshments (perhaps the RTE canteen could help here) and pretend to be
pruning roses or rehearsing in the garden when the coach stops. As you
would know which of the stars is more likely to be in need of a weekly
financial windfall, perhaps you would suggest a couple of names.

    Yours sincerely,

    John Mackay

    Mr John Mackay

    PS Congratulations on the Euorovision: douze points!

Dublin 4, Ireland
Telephone 01 643111
Telefax 01 643080
Telex 93700
Direct Line 01 64

Baile Átha Cliath 4, Éire
Telefón 01 643111
Telefax 01 643080
Teleics 93700
Líne Díreach 01 64

Radio Telefís Éireann

4th June, 1993

Mr. John McKay,

Salem Court,
Maxwell Road,
D u b l i n, 6.

Dear Mr. McKay,

Thank you for your letter of 25th May to the Director General regarding your
experience in California and your proposal for Star Tour Eireann Limited.
I regret that it is not our practice to provide the home addresses of any of our
broadcasters or indeed to intrude in any way on their privacy.   For that reason,
your scheme, which I know is operated in the Hollywood area, and indeed some
years ago in Dallas, would not be appropriate in the more personal neighbourhood of Dublin.

Yours sincerely,

Robert K. Gahan,
Assistant Director General

Salem Court
Maxwell Road
Dublin 6

2 March 1993

Mr Ben Dunne
Dunnes Stores
Georges Street
Dublin 2

Dear Ben,

I hope you will forgive my over-familiarity using your first name, but since that Florida carry-on last year, I feel I have known you intimately. Of course I also felt I knew your late father, a pioneering lion of retailing, but never felt the need to show solidarity with him.

Ben, I'll not mince my words: you handled the whole Orlando business like a man. Not for you the cowardly Bishop Casey cut-and-run, grab-a-plane, disappear and then silence. No Ben, you squared up to your problems in the way you run your business: Ben Dunne's better valour beat them all!

The whole business, and I'm not talking about the hotel, flights and other expenses of the February trip, must have set even you back a bit. Lawyers like Mr Butch Slaughter and his partner, according to the media hyenas, "Come expensive or they don't come at all!" Then there was the month in the Betty Ford Clinic in London. And, without prying into your family affairs, Im sure Mrs Dunne needed the occasional box of chocolates and a night out at the pictures.

Everybody says you have no money worries, but then others claim a person can neither be too slim or too rich. And Ben, although your friends may not have the nerve to tell you, "snake hips" is unlikely to be your nickname. But from the many nuggets of wisdom and standing-stones of philosophy you have delivered since the Orlando Incident, I detected a burning desire in you to help others and to let your plight be seen as an example that others may not have to follow.

To encourage you to fight the good fight I enclose a token donation - please let me know how I can help in your worthy quest.

Yours sincerely,

John Mackay

Mr John Mackay

Ben Dunne
c/o Dunnes Stores
Georges Street
Dublin 2

Salem Court
Maxwell Road
Dublin 6

18 October 1993

Dear Ben,

Never a dull moment - out of the Orlando frying pan, and into the mother
of all family fueds. Ben, I sent you a fiver last March, and now I've
a plan that could help both of us make a few pounds.

Like the Dunnes, I have structured my family as a limited liability
company - I am chairman and chief executive of Mackay plc. We do a bit
of this and that: dogfood bowls, commemorative statues and whatever else
we can turn into an earner.

My wife Dympna is company secretary and doubles up as the Mackays'
Margaret Heffernan, combining her financial acumen with a commendable
zeal for charity fundraising (she is currently organising a series of
coffee mornings to help pay off the national debt).

However, for reasons we have yet to fathom, Mackay plc has yet to break
into the billion pound big league. Maybe we're just not tough enough -
Dympna has never taken away my office keys, and I've never even stubbed
my toe in her mineral water.

But anyway, at our last board meeting, we thought: why not ask Ben to
join the board of Mackay plc? At best, we could make the breakthrough
to the big league - at worst, it would at least liven up our board meetings,
which haven't been the same since we suspended Dympna's mother, Maisie,
after the unfortunate incident with the cider and the Actifed on the
balcony of the Stephens Green shopping centre last year.

What do you think, Ben? An earner for all of us!
We look forward to hearing from you, and to the start of a mutually
profitable business relationship.

Yours sincerely,

John Mackay

Mr John Mackay
Chairman and Chief Executive
Mackay plc

Salem Court
Maxwell Road
Dublin 6

25 May 1993

Managing Director
Ulster Bank
Southern Regional Office
College Green
Dublin 2

Dear Sir,

Congratulations on your current radio advert where the young lassie comes into your bank to open an account - but leaves, all in a fuss and a dither, her pretty little mind distracted by thoughts of marriage to the man behind the counter. I have not laughed so much since the FitzWilliam tennis club reaffirmed their men-only status!

Sir, the modern "trendy" media will no doubt slam us as being "sexist" and "out of touch", but you and I both know that sustaining the economy is A MAN'S JOB, and that WE ARE NOT HELPED IN RESTORING SANITY TO THE MARKET by women leaving the kitchen to try to be men.

Things have gone from bad to worse since women were allowed to sign their own cheques and buy their own houses, and you have, in my humble opinion, courageously made this unpopular point with forceful subtlety and good humour.

In the circumstances, I'll move my account from its current Merchant Bank to Ulster Bank immediately - societal stability supercedes short-term profit, and even Merchant Banks now EMPLOY WOMEN who would have access to my private fiscal details. Please send me the relevant forms to transfer my account, and I look forward to a mutually rewarding business relationship.

Yours sincerely,

John Mackay

Mr John Mackay

♻ Ulster Bank Limited

Southern Regional Office
PO Box 145, 33 College Green, Dublin 2
Telephone (01) 777623 Telex 93638
Fax (01) 775035

A member of the National Westminster Bank Group

John Mackay Esq

Salem Court
Maxwell Road
Dublin 6

27 May 1993
Our ref: HS\CH

Dear Mr Mackay

Thank you for your letter of 23 May addressed to the Managing Director which has been passed to me for attention.

To open an account I feel it would be best if you called to the most convenient branch of the Bank. This would enable us to ascertain your exact requirements and complete the formalities.

Thank you for your interest in Ulster Bank and I look forward to being of service to you.

Yours sincerely

HAROLD STRONG
Marketing Manager

Registered in Northern Ireland No. R733. Registered Office: 47 Donegall Place, Belfast BT1 5AU

Salem Court
Maxwell Road
Dublin 6

Bishop Comiskey
Bishop of Ferns
Wexford

23 Feb 1993

Dear Bishop Comiskey,

My heartfelt prayers and sympathy are with you and your fellow-Bishops in this trying time that has stayed on our shoulders since Bishop Casey's temptation by Satan. The good Bishop, who God has forgiven, is quite right to retreat from the media's glare while atoning for his sins.

I could have wept as the media monster then rounded on your good self to satiate its Satan-inspired blood-lust. Unless they can find a child allegedly fathered by your good self, the media should concentrate their column-inches on real moral issues, like the foisting of abortion information on Ireland by the Euro-mandarins of Maastricht.

I do not for one instant believe that your good self would succumb to the sins of the flesh - why else would Bishop Casey have chosen you in whom to confide his problems, if he did not know you were a man beyond temptation who could deal objectively with such issues?

However, as my good wife has told me more than once in recent days, we would not have believed the truth of Bishop Casey's sins had not the media found the child because of Bishop Casey's praiseworthy reluctance to borrow yet again from Diocesan funds.

I therefore enclose a token donation towards any funding you no doubt do not need in this delicate area. Also, what arrangements should I make to contribute regularly by standing order? I know it is not much - I don't have a diocese - and I do not for an instant believe that you will need it, but it makes me feel useful to have sent it.

Yours sincerely,

John Mackay

Mr John Mackay

PS I must also say how much I enjoyed your excellent paperback "It Could Happen to a Bishop" - although perhaps unfortunately named in the context of the still-vivid Galway situation, it is an easily read yet deceptively inspirational font of both faith and wisdom.

Your wicked yet poignant sense of fun permeates every page, shattering the dour and dowdy Hierarchical stereotype beloved of the "liberal" media. Please write more - and to me!

March 1, 1993

Mr. John Mackay

Salem Court
Maxwell Road
Dublin 6

Dear John,

Thank you for your letter of 23 February, 1993 and for the enclosed kind offering.

I regret to say that, in my case, at any rate, it was not so much the national media as the Apostolic Nuncio's error in revealing my name as a go-between in the sad saga of Bishop Casey that caused so much misunderstanding and distress.

What has happened to Bishop Casey is a great tragedy for all concerned. We are all sinners in a very real sense but your offering, while gratefully received, is irrelvant in my case and will go, with your kind permission, to the education of priests and seminarians of which we have a great abundance, thanks and praise to God.

"It could happen to a Bishop" was published two years before Bishop Casey's departure. Obviously they had some left-over copies which they put back on the shelves in the hope that potential buyers might think the book was about Bishop Casey. Thank you for your kind and encouraging remarks about same.

And thank you for your support, generosity and good humour.

God's blessings on you and yours.

Yours sincerely,

+BL

Bishop of Ferns

Mr John Major
Prime Minister
10 Downing Street
London SW1
England

Salem Court
Maxwell Road
Dublin 6

30 July 1993

Dear Prime Minister,

So they say you're dull. So what? Neville Chamberlain was neither a sparkling raconteur nor an irrepressible wit, dinner with Mahatma Gandhi was always something of a trial, and Oscar Wilde had all his best lines scripted by a local wag in a Dublin pub.

Hang in there, John - you turned social convention upside down when you ran away from the circus to become an accountant. You will do so again by making clowns of the ideological acrobats who form the Tory rebel rump.

Not too long ago, our own Prime Minister was also languishing poll-wise. I have since advised him to ignore the pseudo-sophisticates of the media elite. The good news: Albert is now top-dog again - as you can also be by judicious implementation of The Albert Formula.

1   Shut up as often as you can, and keep out of the public eye - the less we see of Albert, the more popular he is. If you must face the media, use popular earthy profanities such as your recent "bastard" speech. Consider borrowing Albert's famous catch-phrase: "crap, total crap".

2   Travel abroad often, then come back and announce that you have won thousands of foreign jobs for Britain. Albert's Jobs-Per-Week-Abroad Ratio is so impressive that Michael Noonan, a popular comedian on our opposition benches, has calculated that if Albert stayed abroad for ever, we would solve our unemployment problem!

3   The EC - your biggest strategic flaw, and the key to The Albert Formula. Ask them _for_ money, don't give it _to_ them. Our Euro-Cash-Per-Head Ratio would see Britain good for over £120 billion - enough for a His and Hers Euro-tunnel and some left over to shut up Thatcher.

As it happens, I'll soon be moving to London and, naturally, I'll be joining the Conservatives. Please send details on signing up - I enclose a token donation to the Party to underline my commitment.

Yours sincerely,

John Mackay

Mr John Mackay

1O DOWNING STREET
LONDON SW1A 2AA

13th August 1993

Dear Mr Mackay,

Thank you for your letter to the Prime
Minister of 30th July. I have been asked to reply
on his behalf.

Mr Major is very grateful for your message
of support and thank you for your donation.

Yours sincerely,

Lucy Miller.

MISS LUCY MILLER
Political Office

J Mackay Esq

Enc

Salem Court
Maxwell Road
Dublin 6

Dr Conor Cruise O'Brien
Whitewater
The Summit .
Howth
County Dublin

26 July 1993

Dear Dr O'Brien,

Although you now seem to confine your public utterances and writings to mundane matters like international affairs and ticking off local politicians, I wish to consult you regarding your principal discipline, medicine, and your speciality, tropical diseases.

I understand you worked in west Africa for some years, in the Congo, and later in Ghana where, I believe, you held a teaching position at a university hospital.

Since my recent return from a visit to the tropics I have noticed that, if I spend any time in the sunshine without full attire, a rash not unlike german measles (but more patchy, and more itchy) develops on my upper body and legs.

I had, of course, sunbathed in Ireland prior to my tropical sojurn, but my dermitological condition only developed, it seems to me, as a direct result of my exposure to an exotic climate.

I have tried every available chemist-shop medication without success and, sadly, my local quack seems to know as much about tropical medicine as he does about international affairs, so you are my "last chance saloon", as they now say.

When you were in the bush, did you discover any folk remedies for such a malady; some lotion, potion, or ointment, brewed up by the local witch doctors from leaves or insects or other "natural" ingredients, which would relieve the irritation and discomfort?

Dr O'Brien, I enclose £5 for this initial consultation. Do you still take private patients?

Yours sincerely,

John MacKay

Mr John MacKay

Salem Court
Maxwell Road
Dublin 6

3 June 1993

Mr Brian Cowen
Minister for Telecom Eireann
Leinster House
Dublin 2

Dear Mr Cowen,

Just two things: your planned phone charge increases and Telecom's much-publicised "phone watch" burglar alarm business.

The "phone watch" advert asks decent people to spend hundreds of pounds on a Telecom burglar alarm to protect their goods.

To me, your planned phone charge increases seem a way of robbing people without the bother and risk of breaking into their homes.

Cowen, I give up. I enclose a fiver; give it to Telecom. It will save them the trouble of dreaming up another fool scheme to enrich a bloated state monolith at my expense.

Yours sincerely,

John Mackay

Mr John Mackay

PS Have your planned phone increases appeared on Crime Line yet?

PPS Don't make that call!

Salem Court
Maxwell Road
Dublin 6

Mr Brian Cowen   26 July 1993
Minister for Aer Lingus
Leinster House
Dublin 2

Dear Mr Cowen,

   Although you didn't acknowledge it, I sent you a fiver for Telecom in
June as a reward for your herculean efforts promoting the phone charge
hikes. I hope they spent it wisely - and not on crippling corporate
buildings in Ballsbridge that cost even more than a phone bill!
   You will be pleased to hear that you have won the Mackay fiver of the
month for August on account of your no-nonsense demolition job on the
national airline. Split it with Cahill if you have to, but if you keep
it yourself (another tough decision) I won't tell him.
   If you would like September's tenner for your hat-trick, turn your
Ministerial bulldozer in the direction of Donnybrook and level RTE's
playing field.

   Yours sincerely,

   John Mackay

   Mr John Mackay

   PS Look up, it's Aer Lingus? Look out, It's Cowen and Cahill!

6 August, 1993.

Mr. John McKay,

Salem Court,
Maxwell Road,
Dublin 6.

Dear Mr. McKay,

On behalf of the Minister for Transport, Energy and Communications, Mr. Brian Cowen, T.D., I wish to acknowledge receipt of your recent letter and enclosure of postal order regarding Telecom Eireann.

I will bring your letter to the Minister's attention.

Yours sincerely,

Eugene Coughlan,
Private Secretary.

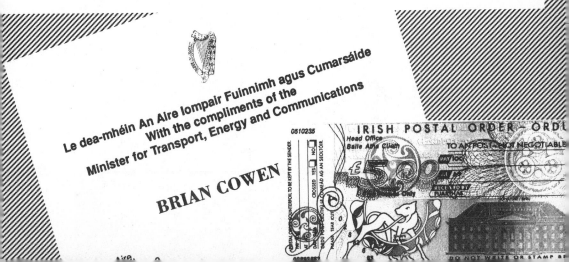

Le dea-mhéin An Aire Iompair Fuinnimh agus Cumarsáide
With the compliments of the
Minister for Transport, Energy and Communications

BRIAN COWEN

IRISH POSTAL ORDER – ORD...
0510235
Head Office
Baile Átha Cliath
£5.00
TO ANY POST... NOT NEGOTIABLE

Salem Court
Maxwell Road
Dublin 6

25 May 1993

Managing Director / Editor
Brandon Books,
Cooleen, Dingle,
County Kerry

Dear Editor,

I greatly enjoyed your book of poems by Michael D Higgins. It has inspired me to write the following three poems - perhaps you would consider including them in a future anthology.

The first is an unattainable quest to capture the very uncapturability of Minister Higgins' unique politico-cultural essence.

It is titled "<u>MICHAEL D</u>":

>   michael d, michael d.
>   nonconformability.
>   poignancy.
>   potpourri.
>   michael d, michael d.

The second is a satirical attempt to combine the reality of unsavoury language with the harsh "empathy-deficit" of Irish feminism.

It is titled "<u>THE TRENDY BORN PERSON</u>":

>   "SPUC? Fuck SPUC!"
>   Said the trendy <u>BORN</u> person.

The third, paradoxically, is a celebration of that same feminism and illustrates the diversity of Irish socio-political thought.

It is titled "<u>SEX-CHANGE TECHNOLOGY</u>":

>   We now have the sex-change technology
>   To give you a womb
>   And let you experience
>   The wonders of child-birth...
>   "Go fuck yourself" said the <u>MAN</u>.

What do you think? I'd appreciate any (constructive!) feedback. How many more poems should I write? Can you publish them? I'm checking with Minister Higgins about getting tax-free status before publication.

Again, congratulations on your (literally!) inspirational book.

Yours sincerely,

John Mackay

John Mackay

BRANDON

Brandon Book Publishers Ltd., Dingle, Co. Kerry, Ireland. Tel. (066) 51463; Fax. (066) 51234
Leabharfhoilsitheoirí Bhréanainn Teoranta, Daingean Uí Chúis, Co. Chiarraí, Éire.

John Mackay

Salem Court
Maxwell Road
Dublin 6

4 June 93

Dear John Mackay

Your comments and congratulations regarding Michael D. Higgins's poetry were most gracious and we were flattered to receive them: would that the paying public always voiced its opinions with such eloquence! We also note with interest the poetic flow which our book inspired in you, and can only urge you to greater effort in this respect. May I suggest you also consult the works of another of our authors, Donall MacAmhlaigh, particularly the story of poet and building labourer Schnitzer O'Shea, wherein he writes:

Am I

the I

I

think

I

am?

Capturing "a deep metaphysical notion... with the minimum of words" (Fr. Alban O Galloglaigh, *Maynooth Magazine*). this poem is known to have a profound consciousness-raising effect when recited. mantra like. in a deep dark room. You might investigate the practicality of constructing a cellar in Salem House where you could practice chanting (allowing ample space for the expanding consciousness, naturally) and, indeed, why not importune Minister Higgins about getting tax concessions on this investment? Perhaps it could be sanctioned as Arts Infrastructure?

Yours very sincerely

Peter Malone

Directors: B. Goggin, S. MacDonogh. Registered No. 87390 in Ireland

Salem Court
Maxwell Road
Dublin 6

Mr Raymond Monahan
President
Incorporated Law Society of Ireland
Blackhall Place
Dublin 7

25 May 1993

Dear Mr Monahan,

Clearly we need to do something. It seems that hardly a day passes
without some solicitor finding themselves caught, as my dear wife Dympna
so delicately puts it, "in financial flagrante delicto." Mr Monahan, this
is causing your people an horrific public relations problem, but it is
still just a matter of perception. So don't panic!

It cannot have escaped your attention that the Solicitor's Bill
proposed by our Bossy Boots justice Minister, Maire Gorgan-Quinn, wants
the solicitors of Ireland to shell out £100,000 for some self-styled
"independent ombudsman" to deal with complaints against themselves.
Sounds to me like the Red Chinese who bill the next of kin for the price
of the bullet used to execute a family member.

Mr Monahan, what you need is high powered public relations to return
the solicitor to his respected perch in Irish society. Is the solicitor
not a bulwark against blackguardism, a sensible man, often smoking a pipe
and having a quiet G agus T with the TD or county surgeon in the rural
golf club? Is the solicitor not a trusted family friend proferring wise
counsel for modest fees. Does the community he serves not place him
somewhere above the bank manager and the accountant, vying with the canny
GP and hard on the heels of the Catholic Bishop?

It would, I presume, be impossible to become President of all the Irish
solicitors without "cop on" and by now you will have cottoned on to my
pitch for your PR contract.

As President, you probably have the "clout" to steer my contract through
your governing committee with a minimum of fuss. You may need to buy a
few drinks for suspicious stick-in-the-muds with votes on the committee,
so I enclose £5 as a down-payment on "expenses". If you need to top up
on "walking around money", just tip a wink.

Mr Monahan, we'll need to meet to discuss the campaign in more detail
- anywhere you suggest is okay by me but I think in the current climate
we should avoid the Shelbourne?

Yours sincerely,

John Mackay

Mr John Mackay

The Incorporated
Law Society of Ireland
Blackhall Place
Dublin 7
Telephone +353-1-6710711
Fax +353-1-6710136

THE LAW SOCIETY

**From the office of
the President**

Mr. John Mackay,

Salem Court,
Maxwell Road,
Dublin 6.

RTM/PD

28th May, 1993

Dear Mr. Mackay,

I am in receipt of your letter of the 25th of May and the enclosed postal order which I now return.

We have in recent years in the Law Society appointed our own Public Relations and Media Officer and are very satisfied with the general improvement in public relations and exposure that has resulted. We have therefore no requirement for the service which you offer.

Yours sincerely,

**RAYMOND T. MONAHAN
PRESIDENT**

Encl.

Des Hanafin
Ex Fianna Fail
Castle Park, Thurles
County Tipperary

23 Feb 1993

Dear Mr Hanafin,

Satan may have won the battle to cast you from the Seanad, Beelzebub, through his agent Reynolds, may have expelled you from the Party which I have supported all my life, but the Fianna Fail faithful, through you, will save Ireland from sex.

You shouted Stop! — but nobody listened. Now, Albert and his new Socialist bedfellows are preparing to promote abortion, divorce, unnatural acts, fornication and adultery - something of a Full House of mortal sins.

It is time for drastic action, but it is inevitable: we need a new political party - with a new but experienced leader of the moral calibre of your good self. I would suggest the "Christian Republicans" as an initial working title.

You may be aware that some small Christian parties contested the last local elections in Dublin. Think how much stronger such a vote would be with the clout of an established religious "heavyweight" such as your good self at its helm.

Such a venture would provide a much-needed political focus for outraged Christians - continuity between referenda, a clarion cry for Christian Ireland in this era of Euro-pagan decadence, and a nationwide campaign to retain Articles 2 and 3 of the Constitution.

It is not too soon to consider an apt "logo" for the Christian Republicans - the symbol of the Christian fish juxtaposed with a lion and a shamrock may, I feel, give the appropriate subliminal messages.

I enclose a token donation towards starting the venture should you choose to do so.

Yours sincerely,

John Mackay

Mr John Mackay

The Sultan of Brunei
Sultan's Palace
Brunei

Dear Sultan,

I am not writing to you on behalf of my government who are proud, elected representatives. No, I write directly on behalf of my fellow citizens, an impoverished nation sitting on the periphery of north-eastern Europe, at the edge of the cold Atlantic ocean.

Try as they may, our government has been unable to get off the carousel of poverty and borrowing, despite joining the European Community and paying dues to the World Bank. Brunei, according to an encyclopaedia, is a wonderful land, warm and inviting, where your people enjoy an idyllic life basking in the benificence of your generosity.

Sultan, I'll be blunt. If you could find your way to giving Ireland, say, thirty billion of our Irish pounds, it would more than cancel our national debt and allow a once proud nation to walk tall with our heads high again. Do you do this sort of thing?

I suppose, like applying for a mortgage to some institutions, there may be a fee for processesing this request, and I enclose £5 for your immediate expenses.

Yours sincerely,

John Mackay

John Mackay

Salem Court
Maxwell Road
Dublin 6

11 June 1993

The Producer
Questions and Answers
RTE, Donnybrook
Dublin 4

Dear Producer,

I have studied your programme over the past season and believe it has improved, although it still needs "personality", a touch of "glamour", SOME NEW FACES and a few laughs. That's the diagnosis, this is the cure:

You need more couples on the panel and, at the risk of sexism, let them be handsome men and lovely women. I still turn out okay in a dark suit and, while Dympna cunningly disguises her body bountiful in a "Demis Roussos" kaftan, she has the face of an angel. Get couples like us and watch the ratings soar!

The formula needs updating too. Why not take turns for spouses to be in a sound-proof booth while the question is asked, then compare the political answer to that which the "other half" believes their partner WOULD give. In viewer-land we call this the hypocrite detector. And why keep it to current events — past affairs might be more interesting for the audience AND keep the panel on their toes!

Get rid of John Bowman — he is too intelligent, and HE DOESN'T ANSWER HIS LETTERS (I wrote to him TWICE asking why the young Green TD Trevor Sargent was put in the audience instead of the panel, and Bowman appears to have pocketed my stamps on BOTH occasions). If he is a doctor, let him go on the Gay Byrne Show and answer questions on healthy living, using his ready wit to quip at Gay, "When you joined RTE you had nothing, now you have piles. More roughage, Mr Byrne, and you'll be sitting comfortable for the rest of your life!"

Get Brush Shields or a "character" to chair Q agus A. Bring it closer to the people. Have U2 or somebody do an upbeat theme tune. Ask guest artists like Chris de Burgh and his Lady In Red onto the panel, then insist they do a duet. What about Shay Healy? He did clever jokes on the TV, he's on the payroll already, so think of the licence payers. Wit and wisdom at no extra cost; ratings soar to Eurovision levels.

I have many more ideas, so if you want us to get together, just drop me a line.

Yours sincerely,

John Mackay

John Mackay

PS Any chance of a pair of audience tickets?

RADIO TELEFÍS ÉIREANN
DONNYBROOK,
DUBLIN 4,
IRELAND.
TEL: (01) 642945, (01) 642941
FAX: (01) 643087

John MacKay

Salem Court
Maxwell Road
Dublin 6

17 June 1993

Dear John,

Thank you very much for your interesting letter of June 11th. I'm always glad to get feedback and ideas for developing the programme format. I am enclosing tickets for the audience this coming Monday if you wish to attend.

Yours sincerely,

Betty Purcell
Editor
Questions and Answers

QUESTIONS
AND
ANSWERS

QUESTIONS
AND 2 1 JUN 1993
ANSWERS

Mondays at 6.15 pm
Television Studios,

Oifig an Taoisigh
Office of the Taoiseach

Ref: FO/35.

18 March, 1993.

Mr. John Mackay,

Salem Court,
Maxwell Road,
Dublin 6.

Dear John,

In the absence of the Taoiseach, Mr. Albert Reynolds, T.D., who is abroad at present on Government business, I enclose herewith a letter received from Mr. Kieran McGowan, Managing Director, Industrial Development Authority of Ireland, in response to representations the Taoiseach made on your behalf.

The Taoiseach hopes this clarifies matters for you.

Yours sincerely,

Private Secretary.

IDA IRELAND

INDUSTRIAL DEVELOPMENT
AUTHORITY OF IRELAND

Mr. Albert Reynolds T.D.
An Taoiseach
Department of An Taoiseach
Government Buildings
Dublin 2

WILTON PARK HOUSE
WILTON PLACE
DUBLIN 2 IRELAND
TELEPHONE (01) 686633
FACSIMILE (01) 603703

KIERAN McGOWAN
MANAGING DIRECTOR
CHAIRMAN OF EXECUTIVE BOARD

12 March 1993

Dear Taoiseach

I refer to the note from Mr. Jim Stafford of 10 March 1993 regarding the letter you received from Mr. John Mackay, Salem House, Salem Court, Maxwell Road, Dublin 6.

I have also received a letter from Mr. Mackay and have attached, for your information, a copy of my reply.

Mr. Mackay is not planning to manufacture the dog bowls himself. He is primarily interested in ascertaining the viability of producing the bowls and also of seeing if we can identify any company that would manufacture them on his behalf.

The best way forward is for one of my colleagues to meet with Mr. Mackay and go through all the possible options. To this end I have arranged for Mr. Colm MacFhionnlaoich to contact Mr. Mackay to arrange such a meeting.

Yours sincerely

Salem Court
Maxwell Road
Dublin 6

Michael Noonan TD
Leinster House
Dublin 2

2 July 1993

Dear Mr Noonan,

Your meteoric political rise since your electoral promotion to Leinster
House has firmly established you as the REAL Michael Noonan. It is only
a matter of time before you are chosen to lead Fine Gael; you have the
tenacity, sharpness and presence to turn the sinking ship around into
the harbour of competence. I wish you well, and enclose a token donation
to your electoral fighting fund.

Like you, I fully support the compulsory Shannon stopover. Anyone who
can afford to fly to America can afford to spend a few hours spending
their IRISH-EARNED money in what is unfortunately one of Ireland's most
underdeveloped and economically backward regions. They may drain the
Shannon, but they'll never drain the Shannon stopover!

Don't get me wrong; I want to see Aer Lingus saved but, if Dublin has
failed the airline, then the jobs should go in Dublin. The whingeing
Jackeens, who always get everything, must now be told (sympathetically
but firmly) that they can't keep up with the Bransons by dragging the
Shannons down to their own incompetent level.

However, I have a suggestion which could make everyone happy. Why not
transfer the CONCEPT of the Shannon stopover to Dublin? It seems that
most of the job losses will hit north of the Liffey, so I would propose
the following guidelines for the "Northside Stopover":

(1) Every train or bus travelling to Dublin must first stop for half
    an hour on the north side of the city, where the occupants must
    disembark and purchase something (this is deliberately somewhat
    less stringent than the lengthier Shannon stopover);

(2) FOR A TRIAL PERIOD, every person who lives AND works on the south
    side of Dublin, must travel ONCE A WEEK to the north side and
    purchase something.

What do you think? I look forward to hearing your opinion - and to your
inevitable elevation to the Fine Gael Leadership.

Yours sincerely,

John Mackay

Mr John Mackay

DÁIL ÉIREANN
BAILE ÁTHA CLIATH, 2.
(Dublin, 2)

7 July, 1993

Mr. John Mackay,

Salem Court,
Maxwell Road,
Dublin 6

Dear John,

Thank you very much for your recent letter and for your kind comments.

As you know, the Fine Gael Motion on Aer Lingus was debated this week in Leinster House, and the Government was seriously embarrassed during the debate. Sile De Valera and Tony Killeen resigned from the Fianna Fail Party, as did all the Fianna Fail Councillors in County Clare. The Government has accepted Mr. Cahill's proposal to change the Shannon Stopover, and I fear that this will cause serious economic damage to the Mid-West region.

I enclsoe a copy of a speech I made in the Dail on Tuesday night, in which I set out my attitude to the Cahill plan.

Your proposals for generating extra economic activity in the North side of Dublin are very novel, but I can't see them being greeted with acclaim on the south side.

I would like in particular to thank you for the complimentary remarks which you make about myself, and for the contribution of £5 which you make to the Party.

With every good wish.

Yours sincerely,

MICHAEL NOONAN, T.D.

FINE GAEL SPOKESPERSON
TRANSPORT, COMMUNICATIONS & ENERGY

Paul McGuinness
Manager U2
Principal Management

Salem Court
Maxwell Road
Dublin 6

24 September 1993

Dear Mr McGuinness,

My son Toby is a U2 fanatic, so a thought struck me when he came home from your RDS "gig" and sat flicking TV chanels into the early morning. It's his 23rd birthday soon, and I want to give him an extra special present to top his trip to Trump Tower and Hawaii last year. Like your four, he's musical in his own way - he plays the drums and the slide trombone - and he has recently taken to wearing a baseball cap back-to-front on his head, pink varnish on his fingernails, what I understand to be a "grunge" tee-shirt, and flourescent tights that he says he bought at a Freddie Mercury memorabilia sale but which I suspect came from his sister Suzie's wardrobe.

Mr McGuinness, here's my proposal: with his colourful personality, his interest in making noise and his particular penchant for U2, I thought a stint with your lot in the band might give him a birthday treat he would never forget. How much would it set me back for you take him under your wing for a week of your tour, letting him watch the lads from backstage and maybe "jam" along on the slide trombone when appropriate?

I should warn you that he finds it difficult to accept discipline, and his personal hygiene has his mother distracted. Also, as adolescence seems to have stayed with Toby longer than most lads, if you gather my meaning, it may be better if he could have a room on his own as you travel between concerts.

Please let me know how much such a week-long excursion would cost. I enclose £5 to cover the administrative costs of processing this enquiry.

Yours sincerely,

John Mackay

Mr John Mackay

AWAITING
REPLY

Salem Court
Maxwell Road
Dublin 6

20 October 1993

Commissioner Pee Flynn
EC Commission
Brussels
Belgium
County Europe

Bonjour, Commissioner Pee, mon amee,

Shock! Horror! It seems that our allegedly promised £8 billion Euro begging bowl bonanza may be unravelling! Quelle surprise!

But Albert's rousing rallying cry in the Dail has set the tone for a united national effort against the claw-back - and I'll set the ball rolling with a rewrite of the "Dad's Army" theme tune ("Who do you think you are kidding, Mr Delors, if you think we're on the run?").

Also, I think I may have a breakthrough on the shortfall. Why don't you suggest a compromise to top up our begging bowl?

Although it would be treasonous in Fianna Fail terms to suggest you were ever part of the "Renvyle Set", the former home of blessed Oliver St. John Gogarty, turned hotel, and sometimes haunt of that nice Tara Mines crowd, is in your neck of the woods.

Commisioner Pee, why don't you ask Tara to make up the £500 million shortfall to keep the National Plan on the rails and emerge, once again, as a cool clean hero? There are no dozers when the West's Awake!

Like the "Renvyle Set", I seek no personal remuneration for this brainwave - just a hearty "howaya" from Pee Flynn next time he comes to town.

Yours sincerely,

Jay Mackay

Mr Jay Mackay

AWAITING REPLY

Pee. S. I enclose a fiver to kick-start the campaign!

Pee. Pee. S. I will not tell anybody about our plan, and allow you to bathe in its cerebral magnificence.

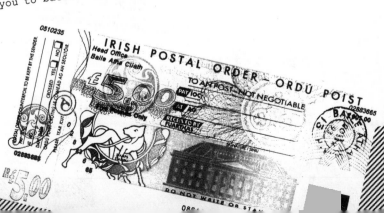

Salem Court
Maxwell Road
Dublin 6

25 May 1993

Michael Colgan
Artistic Director
Gate Theatre
1 Cavendish Row
Dublin 1

Dear Mr Colgan,

Here's a draft outline of a play called "IRELAND". I would appreciate any constructive criticism.

Gearóid and Caitlín go to the theatre to watch a play about the national question (the stage is laid out like a theatre, with another stage and seats). They end up sitting beside Billy and Rhonda, and there is some good-humoured sectarian banter.

In the play they are watching, two balaclava-clad hoods burst into a house to kidnap a Judge until his government gives them back their land. Gearóid and Caitlín cheer. The Judge tells the hoods they must accept the will of the majority. Ian and Rhonda cheer.

At the interval, there is a scuffle in the bar and Gearóid and Billy are mutually hospitalised. Caitlín and Rhonda watch the second half of the play - the Prime Minister rings up the hoods, and agrees to give them back their land. The hoods have won! Caitlín cheers.

Then it turns out that the play they are watching is actually set in the future. Ireland has already been united, and the kidnapped Judge is Irish, not British! The balaclava-clad hoods are actually Loyalists trying to get the Irish government out of Ulster!

"Ho, ho!" laughs Rhonda, "So we won in the end, not you". "Yes" agrees Caitlín, "but neither of us knew whose side we should have been on!". They immediately see the futility of the last 800 years contretemps. They laugh and make up, and go to tell Gearóid and Billy the good news. When they get there, Gearóid kills Caitlín and Billy kills Rhonda for being traitors. The play ends...

What do you think? I've never written a play before. Perhaps you could advise as to how I should proceed further. Do I need a co-writer? Who should I ask to play the various parts? What type of contract should I hold out for? How would you see your own involvement in the production? Do I get advance royalties?

Yours sincerely,

John Mackay

John Mackay

Mr John Mackay   20.8.93

Salem Court
Maxwell Road
Dublin 6

Dear Mr Mackay,

      Thank you for your letter of 10 August, which Michael
Colgan has passed on to me.

      I am afraid that, from the synopsis, it would not seem that
your play Ireland would sit well with the Gate's current
repertoire. Regrettably, the Gate is not in receipt of
sufficient funding to allow for a literary department, or even a
script editor; and so, sadly, we are not in a position to offer
a script development service to authors. The Abbey, on the
other hand, does have a literary department and I wonder if you
have already sent a copy of your synopsis to them?

      I am sorry not to be able to give you better news, and
would like to thank you for your interest in the Gate.

      Yours sincerely,

Anne Clarke
Assistant to Director

THE NATIONAL THEATRE SOCIETY LIMITED

Amharclann na Mainistreach/Abbey Theatre   **An Phéacóg/Peacock Theatre**

Lower Abbey Street Dublin 1
Telephone 8748741/2 Ticket Office 8787222 Fax 8729177

Artistic Director
Garry Hynes
General Manager
Martin Fahy

Directors
James J. Hickey
(Chairman)
Vera Collins
Fedelma Cullen
Michael Doyle

John Fanning
Frank McGuinness
Deirdre Purcell
Carolyn Swift

1 June 1993

Dear Mr Mackay,

In response to your letter to our chairman Mr Hickey let me firstly address your questions. The production of a play, depending on venue, can cost a considerable amount of money. A producer, such as the Abbey, decides whether to present a play based on the finished text. The casting of roles is approached when the play is scheduled into a programme. As to co-writers, this is a matter for yourself as to whom you might wish to work with, or indeed, who might wish to work with you. The contract between producer and writer can take many forms; usually the writer's agent discusses such matters.

It is very difficult to make any assessment of a potential play based on an outline. In the absence of any knowledge of any other work you may have produced in other forms (short story or novel), we can only look at the plot outline and question its theatricality.

The audience are watching an audience who are watching a play. This suggests itself as an idea more televisual than theatrical; the need to get close and observe the behaviour of the audience members without disturbing the process of the play within the play. If an audience member interjects they are usually asked to remain quiet, otherwise their outburst must be acknowledged by the preformers in the play. A tangible dialogue between audience and performers could be effective and interesting, but would totally disrupt the plot of the play within the play. This would introduce an entirely different dynamic to the one you propose.

I am afraid the only way we could be of positive help would be to explore the play when you have written it. I thank you for contacting our theatre and wish you the very best with the work.

Yours sincerely,

David Byrne
New Writing Editor

Mr Ross Perot
United We Stand America
12377 Merit drive
Dallas, Texas 75251

Salem Court
Maxwell Road
Dublin 6
Republic of Ireland

11 July 1993

Dear Mr Perot,

You're Ross, and you're the boss, cutting through the candy floss! Your sound bites of plain talk illuminate an incandescent vision for the future. As you so rightly said of of red tape and bureaucracy: "If you see a snake, you kill it, you don't form a Committee to talk about it!" Sadly, in Ireland, we would form a Committee and elect the snake as chairman.

It seems clear you will challenge President Clinton in 1996, but could I suggest a fall back position? In 1997 the Irish President, Mrs Mary Robinson, is up for re-election. I think you would walk in. Don't worry about nationality; we had an American citizen as President before, and he had the added disadvantage of a Spanish name.

I had thought of running myself but I believe you would have a novelty value (and a monetary one). I believe I would be a useful foil as Vice President — something of an Irish Admiral Stockdale. Although I never served in the military, my son Tobias knows a lot of sailors and he could show me the ropes, so to speak.

I also hear that your company, Perot Systems, is seeking to use the emerald isle as a foothold to launch a data information system in Europe. If I could be of any assistance regarding elementary industrial espionage, it would be an honour to serve.

Ross, don't let the political pygmies dwarf your vision for a better tomorrow. My son Tobias has just attained a coveted visa to move to America, and he plans to play his part in your United We Stand campaign. Please send further details — how to join, bank account number for donations etc?

Hip hip hooray, we're on our way, to give Ross the Boss his day!

Yours sincerely,

John MacKay

Mr John MacKay

PS You may be a billionaire, but I've yet to meet any visionary who couldn't make use of some extra green folding stuff, so I enclose a token £5 donation to put towards United We Stand America.

Salem Court
Maxwell Road
Dublin 6

2 March 1993

Dr Michael Smurfit,
Chairman,
Jefferson Smurfit Group,
Dublin

Dear Dr Smurfit,

We do not deserve you and if you were to stay in Monaco and not come back here at all it would serve us right. Shame, shame, shame on those who impugned your reputation and made you a target for an "investigation" which is obviously modelled on a Soviet-style show trial.

You must have noticed that the fundamentalists who have imposed their vertiginous standards of rectitude on the happy-go-lucky Irish people are as allergic to the penicillin of the free market as the late Count Dracula was to sunlight. It is hardly a coincidence that the inquisition on the Commandos of Capitalism began soon after the crash of international communism.

Those of us who were there will never forget your revolutionary attempt at egalitarianism in the equestrian world, Classic Thoroughbreds, a glorious attempt to give the common man an opportunity to walk alongside the Captains and Kings in the winners' enclosure. It failed, but it was a beautiful failure.

Michael Smurfit never cheated at golf. He played the game: he won, he lost. In victory he was magnanimous; in failure, generous.

Your interest in property coalesces with my own! Through the years I have picked up a few title deeds, nothing as spectacular as the Ballsbridge site you spotted for the ingrates at Telecom, but a few handy little plots, some in the middle of stretches of land other entrepreneurs will want to develop. Maybe we could talk about that some time, I could use your wise counsel.

Dr Smurfit, I want to put our relationship on a more formal footing. For that reason I am enclosing £5 to cover the cost of you sending me any information with which I can more comprehensively defend your integrity when challenged by some of my socialistically-hypnotised peers.

Yours sincerely,

John Mackay

Mr John Mackay

Telephone: 2696622
Fax No: 2694481
Telex No: 93411
Telegrams: Smurfit, Dublin

Registered in Ireland No. 8610

Directors:
Dr. M. W. J. Smurfit, *Chairman & Chief Executive*
P. A. Smurfit, *Joint Deputy Chairman*
D. F. Smurfit, *Joint Deputy Chairman*
H. E. Kilroy, FCA, *President & Chief Operations Director*
E. Ryan
W. J. MacDonald, BA, FCA
P. J. P. Gleeson
J. B. Malloy, MA, BS (USA)
D. F. T. Austin
J. M. O'Dwyer, LLB
Dr. T. A. Reynolds, Jr. (USA)
A. P. J. Smurfit, BS
G. E. Gomez, BS, MBA (Colombia)
R. Mac Sharry

Secretary:
M. R. J. Pettigrew, BA, CA

JEFFERSON SMURFIT GROUP plc

Beech Hill, Clonskeagh, Dublin 4

30th March 1993.

Mr. John Mackay,

Salem Court,
Maxwell Road,
Dublin 6.

Dear Mr. Mackay,

Further to your letter of March 2nd, we have no comment to make on the matter and I return herewith your postal order.

Many thanks,

Yours sincereiy,

Ian J. Curley
Personal Assistant
to Dr. M.W.J. Smurfit

Salem Court
Maxwell Road
Dublin 6

18 May 1993

Dr Michael Smurfit
Irish Consulate
Monaco

Dear Dr Smurfit,

I have taken the liberty of writing to you at your Monaco address because
I am convinced that your mail is being being tampered with in Dublin and
that you are not being allowed to see letters from "ordinary" people
like my good self who do not meet certain fiscal standards.

I wrote to you on 2 March 1993 proposing a merging of our interests,
and seeking advice with which to argue your side of the Telecom site
business. Dr Smurfit, someone calling himself "Ian J Curley, Personal
Assistant to Dr MWJ Smurfit", sent me a terse rebuff, returning some
monies which I had intended for you.

Dr Smurfit, I may not possess the outer trappings of a millionaire
lifestyle, but I have my personal integrity; a concept which your Dublin-
based staff seem not to even acknowledge, but one which I am certain you
adhere to in your business and personal life.

I enclose again the token donation which your Mr Curley returned to
me, I repeat the good wishes and moral encouragement which I expressed
in my original letter, and I look forward to a civilised response.

Yours sincerely,

John Mackay

Mr John Mackay

PS Perhaps it might be best if you kept this matter on a need-to-know
basis amongst your Dublin staff.

IRISH POSTAL ORDER – ORDÚ POIST

Justice Hamilton
The Beef Tribunal
Dublin castle
Dublin 2

Salem Court
Maxwell Road
Dublin 6

26 July 1993

Dear Justice Hamilton,

May I begin by congratulating you on your your superb handling of the
Beef Tribunal. Only a man with the wisdom of Solomon, the cuteness of
a cattle dealer and the integrity of Justinian himself could have guided
the nation through such a constitutional and moral labyrinth.
However, I write to ask your assistance on a personal matter. My only
daughter Suzie has been keeping company with an apprentice solicitor and
Mrs Mackay is convinced that wedding bells are in the air.
As you know, on such an occasion, it is incumbent on the bride's father
to foot the bill for whatever festivities and merrymaking in which some
two hundred odd people may see fit to indulge themselves.
While I do not mind paying my dues to Bacchus, the prospect of public
speaking somewhat terrifies me. As one of the great advocates, I could
never hope to match your style and delivery, but your legal background
is undoubtedly a goldmine of anecdotes and experience.
And so to my plea: could you furnish me with a few judge's jokes and
advocate's anecdotes to impress Suzie's future in-laws?
I have heard of a case where a witness, who had been verbally abused
by a neighbour, could not bring himself to repeat the foul-mouthed insult
in open court. The judge asked him to write it down, so he wrote "F**k
off, you dozy b*****d" on a page. The judge, after reading it, passed
it to a court clerk to pass to the barrister. The clerk, who had been
asleep, woke up, read the note, picked up his documents and left!
I also believe there was a case where a German witness could speak no
English, the legal eagles could speak no German, and a man in the public
gallery volunteered to translate. When the Judge asked him to ask the
witness his name, the volunteer smiled and, using a theatrical stage-
German accent, loudly shouted "Vot ist yur name!"
Could you let me know at which cases these incidents happened? I am
sure that you must also know many more such anecdotes and I would be truly
honoured if you could share some with me.

Yours sincerely,

John Mackay

Mr John Mackay

Mrs Jean Kennedy Smith
Ambassador to Ireland
American Embassy
Ballsbridge
Dublin 4

Salem Court
Maxwell Road
Dublin 6

17 August 1993

Dear Ambassador,

Céad míle fáilte. The combined charisma of your good self and our own
President Robinson could light the beacon of an Irish political Camelot,
where the women don't have to push the pram a lot.
    I write to suggest a plan to help strengthen still further the always
excellent relationship between our two nations.
    As you know, next year will see the 25th anniversary of the first
American on the moon. This year Dawson Stelfox led the first Irish
expedition to conquer Mount Everest. Why not commission a statue to
jointly commemorate these historic events?
    My wife Dympna, who has studied art, has drafted the enclosed design
for such a monument, which would be sculpted from granite and sited outside
your newly-renovated Embassy edifice.
    Three specific questions.
    Firstly, could you get your brother Teddy to twist Bill Clinton's arm
for some funding for the statue? Everyone else's fingerprints seem to
be somewhere on the pork barrel!
    Secondly, could you participate in a fund-raising scheme on New Years
Day, in which Mr Stelfox would climb Dublin's Liberty Hall, with rubber
suckers on his hands and feet, and dressed as Spiderman - an appropriately
American icon. You would greet him at the top, attired as Wonderwoman,
another American icon, and present him with a cheque from Bill Clinton
as the Tricolour and the Stars and Stripes fly proudly behind you.
    Thirdly, can you act as Treasurer for the venture? If so, I enclose
£5 to kick-start the account.
    Again, céad míle fáilte.

Yours sincerely,

John Mackay

Mr John Mackay

PROPOSED DRAFT DESIGN FOR
GRANITE STATUE TO JOINTLY
COMMEMORATE FIRST SUCCESSFUL
AMERICAN MOON LANDING AND FIRST
SUCCESSFUL IRISH EVEREST
EXPEDITION

Salem Court
Maxwell Road
Dublin 6

17 August 1993

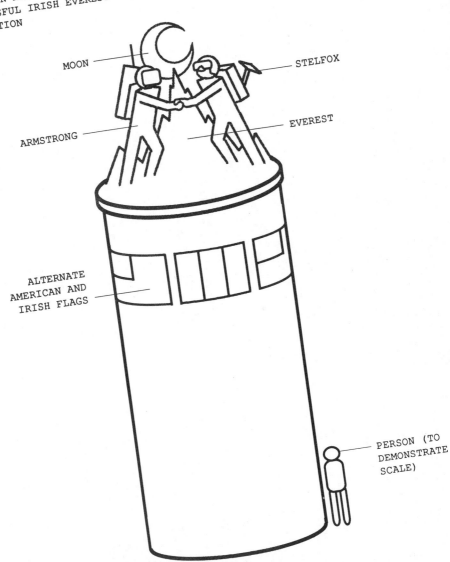

MOON

STELFOX

ARMSTRONG

EVEREST

ALTERNATE
AMERICAN AND
IRISH FLAGS

PERSON (TO
DEMONSTRATE
SCALE)

SUBMITTED TO MRS JEAN KENNEDY SMITH,
AMERICAN AMBASSADOR TO IRELAND,
FOR CONSIDERATION AND POTENTIAL FUNDING

EMBASSY OF THE
UNITED STATES OF AMERICA

Dublin

September 15, 1993

Mr. John Mackay

Salem Court
Maxwell Road
Dublin 6

Dear Mr. Mackay,

Thank you for your recent letter to Ambassador
Smith.

The Ambassador cannot engage in activities such
as acting as treasurer for your venture. I am returning
your £5 check.

Sincerely,

Deidre O'Byrne
Executive Assistant

Enclosure

Mr Liam O Murchu
c/o RTE Television
Donnybrook
Dublin 4

Salem Court
Maxwell Road
Dublin 6

29 September 1993

Mr O Murchu, a chara,

I have always admired your ability to present the Irish language in a "trendy" and "user-friendly" manner, so I felt I should write to you about the following idea.

Watch any Irish soccer match today, and you face a gale of obscene terrace chanting - mostly imported from England. What about a voluntary code of translating the worst of the chants from harsh Anglo-Saxon to our own native tongue in "Trom agus Eadtrom" style?

For example, unpopular decisions by the ref would no longer be met by: "The referee's a bastard, and so say all of us" (ironically rendered to the tune of "for he's a jolly good fellow"). Instead we would hear the undeniably more culturally sensitive: "The ref's a páiste gréinne..." (sung to the same air).

The observation that a player, by virtue of missing an easy goal, is deemed unfit to wipe the nether regions of the chanting spectators would become: "You're not fit to glan mo thóin".

As a humorous "hook", the unfortunately everpopular expletives "f**k" and "f**kin" etc, could be replaced by "doyle" and "doylin" (after the writer Roddy Doyle). This would transform the following overtly aggressive chant, with its accompanying synchronised clapping:

"There's gonna be a nasty accident
(CLAP, clap-clap-CLAP, clap-CLAP, clap-CLAP-clap-clap)
You're going home by f**kin ambulance
(CLAP, clap-clap-CLAP, clap-CLAP, clap-CLAP-clap-clap)"

into the more auditorally pleasant alternative of:

"There's gonna be a diabhlaí timpiste (clap, clap-clap etc)
You're dul abhaile by doylin othercharr (clap clap-clap etc)"

Result? A more pleasant atmosphere, AND a boost for the Irish language. Mr O Murchu, If you will publicly endorse the idea, I will produce an official chant-translation dictionary, which could be distributed at all soccer matches with the aid of a Government grant.

Is mise le meas,

John Mackay

Mr John Mackay

The Secretary
Royal Dublin Golf Club
Portmarnock
County Dublin

Salem Court
Maxwell Road
Dublin 6

11 June 1993

Dear Sir,

After making enquiries, I understand yours is the best golf club in
Dublin not to allow women members so I have decided to join.

As you have no doubt read elsewhere, I have recently returned from
abroad having accumulated some wealth doing this and that. However,
ignore the poisonous gossip columns: everything I did was legal and above
board. Life is ruthless, business competitive, casualties inevitable.
As my wife Dympna says when I allow her speak in company, "John is tough
but scrupulously fair."

Man to man, let me assure you that money will not be an obstacle, so
I expect you can fix it so that the "committeee" or whoever is supposed
to "select" new members will not resort to a premature "Sammy Davis
Junior" which, I understand, the "blackballing" proceedure is sometimes
called. No doubt some of your more conservative colleagues will need some
persuading of my eligability, so I enclose a token down payment on the
cost of a few drinks to "oil" my application.

As I still regularly travel abroad on business I may not be available
at short notice for any interview or appearance before the "committee",
so I would appreciate it if you would clear that in advance.

Yours sincerely,

John Mackay

Mr John Mackay

The Royal Dublin Golf Club

TELEPHONE
CLUBHOUSE 337153
LOCKER ROOM 336085

DOLLYMOUNT
DUBLIN 3

Mr. John Mackay,

Salem Court,
Maxwell Road.
Dublin 6

Dear Sir,   28th June 1993

We acknowledge receipt of your letter of 11th June
concerning membership of the Club.

I am instructed to inform you that the membership files are
closed and I return your Postal Order £5.00 herewith.

Yours sincerely,

P.P. J.A.Lambe.
Secretary/Manager,

SECRETARY J.A. LAMBE TELEPHONE 336346
FAX NO. 336504

Salem Court
Maxwell Road
Dublin 6

17 Feb 1993

Alan Dukes TD
Leinster House
Dublin 2

Dear Mr Dukes,

It is becoming increasingly clear that your political "shafting" was premature. You may not have pandered willy-nilly to the media circus, and you were rebuffed by the electorate for offering the Dungannon-based Austin Currie for President, but how have Fine Gael fared under your successor? Worse, worse, worse.

As you have made quite clear, the problem was not your leadership but the party itself, just as now the problem is not the party but John Bruton's leadership.

I was impressed with John Bruton's televised ard-fheis speech last year. However, I dare say you were even more impressed by the sustained delegate applause which greeted your own elevation to your seat behind the podium. You must have laughed at the delicious irony of it all – would that they had reacted so in the wake of the Tallaght strategy, which John Bruton now praises! Ho ho.

Here's the point. The country is still descending into political and economic chaos, yet the dead and directionless Fianna Fail hand stays heavily on the State tiller. Your responsible statesmanlike approach – so often confused with dullness – must form part of the reshaping of Fine Gael's public image. You must not only return to the front bench, but indeed bide your time until your inevitable return to power.

Having returned to Ireland, I am considering joining Fine Gael. I am also, with some colleagues, considering launching a non-party-political "Bring Back Garret" campaign. While it may not succeed in winning Garret over – let's face it, you couldn't get him to run for President – it could help revive the surging optimism that permeated the party in the eighties. Would you consider advising us on such a venture?

Yours sincerely,

John Mackay

Mr John Mackay

PS In the meantime, may I add that, once I join the party, I will of course be seen to support the current leadership until it changes. I know that you as a man of dignity and loyalty would want nothing less.

DÁIL ÉIREANN
BAILE ÁTHA CLIATH, 2.
(Dublin, 2).

22 February 1993

Dear Mr Mackay

Thank you for your letter of February 17. I am very grateful to you for your kind and encouraging remarks about me.

I am very pleased to hear that you are considering joining Fine Gael. On the basis of your letter, I am quite sure that you will have a very useful contribution to make to informed debate on both policy and strategy within the Party. Of course I understand that as a loyal Party member, you would support the current leadership.

I honestly think that there would be very little point in running a "bring back Garret" campaign. Garret has definitively left the party political arena and I am very strongly of the view that he has given the Party so much that he owes us nothing now. Indeed, we are still in his debt.

We now have to give the Party a new vitality and thrust. This means, in my view, that we have to be a great deal more forthright and sharp in what we say, even at the expense of occasionally coming into conflict with some segments of public opinion and offending some people. I have long believed, in any case, that a substantial proportion of the electorate make up their minds about a party on the basis of an overall view of its performance, and are quite prepared to accept the fact that the Party they support may not always take a line which they find congeniall on every issue. At the end of the day, I believe that they respect determination and clarity.

As far as my own position is concerned, I was brought back to the Front Bench last September as Spokesperson on the Environment. I understand that a re-shuffle is imminent, and I do not know what it will bring. Whatever the result, I intend to maintain the highest profile possible and to do everything I can to strengthen the party's contribution to national politics.

Yours sincerely

ALAN M DUKES TD
URLABHRAÍ COMHSHAOIL

Salem Court
Maxwell Road
Dublin 6

25 May 1993

Mr Frank Feeley
City Manager
City Hall
Dublin 2

Dear Mr Feeley,

I am currently negotiating with RTE, Bus Eireann and a number of other public and private bodies regarding an industry which I would like to set up before this tourist season finishes.

Having recently returned from California and taken a tour of the stars' homes in Hollywood, Bel Air and Beverly Hills, I believe there is enormous potential for the same sort of thing in Dublin.

RTE is expected to provide the "inside info" and addresses of our biggest local personalities and Bus Eireann is bidding to supply a suitable vehicle with toilet facilities. We will provide the driver — who in their right mind would leave a public servant in charge of anything, especially a business in its infancy?

What we expect from Dublin Corporation is the funding of a stars guide map, road signs (directing the coach to each star's home, and also usable for punters who choose to walk the tour) plus suitable plaques for the wall of the houses. This would have to be done immediately.

I would appreciate an early reply, with proposed timescales for carrying out this work.

Yours sincerely,

John Mackay

Mr John Mackay

PS Another query: We expect our coach to have toilet facilities. If this "facility" is used when stationary, should our driver park the coach over a drain or grating?

bárdas áta cliat
(CORPORATION OF DUBLIN)

halla na Catrac
baile Áta Cliat 2

Tel. (01) 6796111
Fax (01) 6798159

CITY HALL
DUBLIN 2
IRELAND

3rd June 1993

Mr. John MacKay,

Salem Court,
Maxwell Road,
Dublin 6.

Dear Mr. McKay,

The City Manager has asked me to acknowledge your letter dated 25th May, 1993.

Dublin Tourism Organisation, on which the Corporation is represented, has a lot of experience in this general area of identifying places of interest to tourists and preparing and signposting trails, such as the heritage trail, the rock trail, and they might best be in a position to advise you. The City Manager has mentioned your proposal to them and I am forwarding your letter and suggesting that they might contact you.

If you think it necessary to provide toilet facilities you will need to have an arrangement within your own premises to discharge sewage via a drain into the public sewer. You should consult in advance with the Divisional Engineer of the Drainage Section, Civic Offices, Fishamble Street, Dublin 8 (Tel. No. as above).

Yours sincerely,

Andrew McHugh
Secretary to City Manager

DUBLIN TOURISM

1 Clarinda Park North, Dun Laoghaire, Co. Dublin, Ireland.
Telephone (01) 2808571. Fax (01) 2802641. Telex 32462 & 93560

June 28th, 1993

Mr John Mackay,

Salem Court,
Maxwell Road,
Dublin 6.

Dear Mr Mackay,

Your letter to the City Manager has been passed for my attention.

I note there is no telephone number on your letter and I would appreciate if you would telephone me over the next few days to set up an appointment to meet.

Yours sincerely,

Patsy O'Connell
Tourism News

Bertie Ahern TD
Minister for Finance
Department of Finance
Merrion Street
Dublin 2

Salem Court
Maxwell Road
Dublin 6

18 May 1993

Dear Mr Ahern,

You are growing apace in stature as the toast of drawing room Dublin 4 following your heroic devaluation of the punt and your chastising of stockbrokers J & E Davy over the Greencore share placement scandal. However, in the midst of the organised chaos, either the postal system has gone awry or some light-fingered lad in your very office has pocketed £5 which I sent to you THREE MONTHS AGO.

My niece was preparing a UCD thesis entitled "Politics and People", and I asked you to verify the authenticity of two anecdotes for inclusion. She has by now drafted the relevant sections thusly:

1. "They call him the anorak man, but he does not hang around with hoods. On Boxing Day itself he braves the snow to hand-deliver Christmas greetings to his grateful constituents. Bah, humbug, moan his opponents – but Bertie delivers, both literally and metaphorically" (page 43, para 3)

2. "Accused that his canvassers were misleading voters by claiming there were no health cuts, an unphased Bertie simply laughed: "ah sure God love them, they're not familiar with the details". The hostility was defused; as always, it was Bertie and the voter against everyone else" (Page 62, para 2)

Bertie, you are a busy man running the economy while Dick and Albert are running scared, so a brief authorisation to include the anecdotes will suffice – though if possible, sooner rather than later; time and tide wait for no thesis.

Yours sincerely,

John Mackay

Mr John Mackay

PS No need for a sworn enquiry on the fiver, though it would be nice to know that it has reached its intended destination. If it hasn't, please let me know and I will send another by return of post.

Salem Court
Maxwell Road
Dublin 6

18 May 1993

Albert Reynolds TD
Taoiseach
Government Buildings
Dublin 2

Dear Albert,

Just a short note to see how you are getting on and to fill you in on the current state of the dogfood bowls project – Mr McGowan has given responsibility at the IDA end to a Mr MacFhionnlaoich (Small Business Division), who seems to know what he is doing. Thanks again for your help, and I will keep you in touch with future developments.

I hope things are going okay with running the country, and I must say you looked great on the telly in Millstreet. Things are grand at my end; Dympna had a bit of a cold last week, but she seems much better now. I'll sign off now, as I am sure you are busy – and able to get some work done, now that the PDs are gone, thank God.

Yours sincerely,

John Mackay

John Mackay

PS I have made clear to Mr McGowan that I wish the project to be treated strictly on its commercial merits. I know that you, as a man of the highest integrity, would want nothing less.

PPS What about Longford for next year's song contest? I'll be visiting my family there next month, and I'll bounce the idea around.

Ref. No. FO/35.

26 May, 1993.

Mr. John Mackay,

Salem Court,
Maxwell Road,
Dublin 6.

Oifig an Taoisigh
Office of the Taoiseach

Dear John,

The Taoiseach, Mr. Albert Reynolds, T.D., has asked me to write to you in response to your recent letter outlining the present position of the dogfood bowls project.

The Taoiseach has asked me to say that he wishes you every success with your project.

Yours sincerely

Private Secretary.

Salem Court
Maxwell Road
Dublin 6

25 May 1993

The Editor
Job News newspaper
Unit 5, Woodpark
Sallynoggin
County Dublin

Dear Editor,

Congratulations! At last, a newspaper devoted entirely to helping people to get a job. I'd love to be involved - is there any chance of a job working on Job News? I'll do anything!

Yours sincerely,

John Mackay

Mr John Mackay

JOBNEWS

Unit 5, Woodpark, Sallynoggin, Co. Dublin. Telephone: 2840858. Facsimile: 2840860.

Mr. J. Mackay,

Salem Court,
Maxwell Road,
Dublin 6.

27/5/93

Dear John,

Than you for taking the time to write to me about JobNews. I'm delighted to hear that you are pleased to see or paper on the shelves and I certainly hope that with the support of you and many more readers we will go from strength to strength.

I appreciate your offer of working for JobNews but I regret to tell you that all our staff have been in place for some weeks prior to the launch and there is no immediate prospects of a vacancy. I am holding your file so that we can refer to you again should something arise in the near future.

I know that is not the answer you would want but I do hope you will understand and hopefully JobNews will be able to deliver the job you are looking for in next weeks issue !

Goood luck in the job hunt,

Brendan Barrett
Publisher.

PS I am returning a stamp to you as it is only fair that you shouldn't be asked to pay for the right of a reply

                                                            Salem Court
                                                            Maxwell Road
Sultan Sir Muda Hasanal   Dublin 6
Bolkiah Mu'izuddin Waddaulah, H.M.,
D.K., D.S.P.N.B., P.S.N.B.,   17 August 1993
P.S.L.J., S.P.B.M., P.A.N.B.,
Sultan of Brunei,
Prime Minister of Brunei,
Sovereign and Chief of Royal Orders
instituted by Sultans of Brunei,
Istana Darul Hana, Brunei,
c/o The Aviary, Osterley, England

Dear Sultan Sir Muda Hasanal Bolkiah Mu'izuddin Waddaulah,

   I wrote to you three months ago suggesting that you consider donating
some of your vast fortune to the Irish government. I was surprised not
to have received a reply, especially since I had enclosed IR£5 to cover
the cost of processing the request.
   However, I now realise that I did not address you by your full title
in my original letter, and it may have therefore been delivered to a
different Sultan instead.
   Since the Irish economy has since gone from bad to worse, I repeat my
penury-stricken plea: Sultan, is there any chance you could find your
way to giving Ireland about thirty billion pounds?
   I look forward to hearing from you, and I again enclose IR£5 to cover
any administrative costs.

   Yours sincerely,

   John Mackay

   Mr John Mackay

Salem Court
Maxwell Road
Dublin 6

17 Feb 1993

Cllr Trevor Sargent TD
Leader, the Green Party
Leinster House

Dear Mr Sargent,

Congratulations on your recent elevation to the Dail. I have only recently been converted to the environmental cause, after viewing a frightening television programme about the dangers of skin cancer. For years, like so many others, I have been blisfully unaware of how much ozone I may be inhaling - no longer! The world owns us, not us the world - yet so few realise it.

Two questions. First, what exactly are you doing in the Dail? Surely the message must be brought directly to the people. I know you have made a start by appearing in the audience instead of the panel on TV shows, but I am thinking of masss demonstrations of ecological activists led by a comely party member dressed as a mermaid extolling the virtues of fresh water, along with your good self as a bald eagle reclaiming the air for Mother Nature.

Secondly, are you associated with the Irish Green Party, based in Clonskeagh, and led by an appropriately named Mr Greene? Perhaps a merger? Unity is strength etc.

At present, however, the "Green" public image remains that of a gaggle of lunatic besandalled idealists, womenfolk sporting "Mother Earth" early-American-settler style dresses, menfolk bedecked in Kelly green cord jackets with suede elbow patches. Unfair? Yes. Real world? Also. Frankly, you could do better than your "young lad in a casual jersey on an old bicycle" image. However uncomfortable it may feel, you are now an important and powerful man. Still, you seem intelligent and eager to learn. That's good.

Three suggestions: Firstly, a more modern yet mature image - suit and tie, good car, and carry an expensive briefcase. Secondly, hard-hitting support for the free market and limiting so-called "worker's rights" could help us move beyond the chaos of "industrialisation". Thirdly, check out the still "trendy" motion picture "Wayne's World", retaining key young-persons "catch-phrases".

If such were to happen, I would be delighted to join the party and indeed to participate in your "handlers" group. As I hope you can tell, I am a man of ideas, at least some of which may be useful to you.

Yours sincerely,

John Mackay

Mr John Mackay

TREVOR SARGENT
37 TARA COVE
BAILE BRIGÍN
CO. ÁTHA CLIATH
FÓN: 01-8412371

DÁIL ÉIREANN
BAILE ÁTHA CLIATH, 2.
(Dublin, 2).

Mr. John Mackey,

Salem Court,
Maxwell Road,
Baile Átha Cliath 6.

22 Feabhra 1993

John, a chara,

You certainly draw an interesting picture of yourself and the Greens. I'd love to meet you sometime, As it so happens, I normally do wear the suit or at least jacket & tie, have a 1990 1 litre car and the briefcase is relatively new too.

Seriously though, you're right about the need to make waves but I wouldn't be so hard on the bicycle. The Netherlands and Denmark are much more in tune with what makes for a good quality of life & bicycles figure very strongly throughout society there. By the way, my appearance on Questions & Answers happened at very short notice (1 hr.) and as the Dáil wasn't sitting I was working casually dressed in my office that day - hence the jumper!

I think from your address that you are near to the group which elected Cllr. John Gormley. Perhaps you could ring him to find out what the Greens are doing locally and what involvement you might like to have. His number at home is 609148 or at work 380122.

Please let me know how you get on.

Beir bua is beannacht,

Trevor

Cllr Trevor Sargent TD
Leader, the Green Party
37 Tara Cove
Baile Brigin

Salem Court
Maxwell Road
Dublin 6

2 Mar 1993

Dear Mr Sargent,

Many thanks for your courteous and prompt response to my recent letter. I'm responding to your home address, which I notice from your letterheading that you prefer to use - the personal touch.

I understand completely that, but for the short notice involved, you would have been more appropriately attired on your recent TV appearance. One the one hand, of course, stay alert, but on the other, what a monstrous imposition to have given you so little notice! Perhaps it would help if I wrote a stinker to RTE?

It's also good to see you on top of both of your jobs, but take some advice from a man of more years than your good self: if one post must suffer, follow the votes, neglect the Dail and protect the Council seat. You need a solid foundation before you can build - with or without planning permission!

May I also say that my teenage daughter Suzie was very impressed with your interview in the popular music magazine "The Hot Press", though my wife was somewhat concerned that you seemed to be downplaying the importance of the environment. I explained that, as a national figure, you must be seen to take "positions" on issues other than those you were elected on. She seemed satisfied with that.

I will of course contact your Mr Gormley, though my time in his area is limited as I am soon moving from the urban greyness of Dublin to a pleasant meadowland near Cork. In the meantime, I would be delighted to meet with you as you suggest. Life's long journey has made me aware that a chat with the man at the top is what counts, whether you are in a multinational conglomerate or a five-house residents committee.

How about the Shelbourne bar? Its pleasant, and it sets the right tone. Would sixish on Monday March 22 suit?

Yours sincerely,

John Mackay

Mr John Mackay

PS I know this is somewhat of an impertinance, but would there be any chance of you signing a photograph of your good self as a birthday surprise for my daughter Suzie? She collects "personality" autographs.

TREVOR SARGENT T.D.
37 TARA COVE
BAILE BRIGÍN
CO. ÁTHA CLIATH
FÓN: 01 412371

THE GREEN PARTY
COMHAONTAS GLAS

DÁIL ÉIREANN
BAILE ÁTHA CLIATH, 2.
(Dublin, 2).

Mr. John Mackey,

Salem Court,
Maxwell Road,
Baile Átha Cliath 6.

10 Márta 1993

Dear John,

I was delighted to receive your letter. Monday 22nd March sounds
fine. Could you make it 5.30 p.m. if possible as I need to head
away again at 6.20 p.m. from the Shelbourne.

I'd be keen to discuss the dual mandate question with you and any
other issues that cross your mind. The signed photograph is
enclosed. There is no accounting for taste. I hope your daughter
isn't too disappointed.

Le gach dea-ghuí,

Cllr. Trevor Sargent T.D.

Salem Court
Maxwell Road
Dublin 6

The Commercial Manager,
Irish Rugby Football Union,   9 March 1993
62 Lansdowne Road,
Dublin 4

Dear sir,

Yes, yes and thrice yes! At last we have won a game, after eleven consecutive defeats. Okay, so Wales were not exactly world class opposition. As Gareth Davies observed, after Wales not so long ago lost seven games out of eight: "the only team we've beaten is Western Samoa – good job we didn't play the whole of Samoa!"

Rugby is a noble sport, misunderstood by the fickle followers of Jack's so-called soccer "Army". Army indeed! When a soccer player trips over his laces, he moans and clutches himself as if increasingly tender parts of his anatomy were being systematically amputated without anaesthetic.

When a rugby man gets knocked inside out by the human equivalent of a furniture removal van, he simply gets up, smiles a toothless smile, wipes the blood and the studs from his wounds, and goes after the man who flattened him to return the compliment fourfold.

Which of these sports is the man's sport? Or does masculinity not count any more? As Arthur Budd put it last century, "a player who could not take and give hacks was not considered worth his salt and to put one's head down in a scrummage was regarded an act of high treason". That such values have not endured is not unconnected with the worldwide collapse in public morality – hanging, not understanding, is what today's criminal needs. I am sure you agree.

Here's the point of my letter. I've recently returned to Ireland after a profitable decade abroad. Now that we're winning again, I'll return to Lansdowne to watch future games – and bring business company. What should I do to book two dozen seats for future games? Need I "pass a few bob" someone's way or will the visible channels suffice? I enclose £5 to cover the cost of processing this request.

Yours faithfully,

John Mackay

Mr John Mackay

PS I cannot overemphasise that I would want top notch seating, away from any soccer riff-raff who may get their dates mixed up.

Irish Rugby Football Union

P. J. O'Donoghue
Secretary and Treasurer

62 Lansdowne Road
Ballsbridge
Dublin 4.
Tel: 684601
Fax: 605640

Ref: 60\POD

15th March, 1993.

Mr. J. MacKay,

Salem Court,
Maxwell Road,
Dublin 6.

Dear Mr. MacKay,

Thank you for your letter of 9th inst.

The normal method of distribution of tickets for international matches at Lansdowne Road is through rugby clubs and schools. However, we are at present renewing ten-year tickets for the East Stand. While existing ticket-holders are being given first preference under the renewal scheme, we are prepared to consider applications from others. Accordingly, I enclose an application for your attention (the amount of £5 forwarded by you is returned herewith).

Yours sincerely,

pf Antoinette Kerry

P. J. O'DONOGHUE
Secretary

Salem Court
Maxwell Road
Dublin 6

23 Feb 1993

Gerry Adams
Sinn Fein, Falls Road
Belfast
North of Ireland

Dear Mr Adams,

I am writing as a devout Christian with a spiritual problem which indirectly concerns you, and on which I hope you can give me some help and advice. I have in recent weeks met a group of inspirational American street preachers called the Society for the Negation of the Power of the Beast. They have explained to me the three major biblical prophetic fulfilments of this age – the birth of the One Lord and Saviour Jesus Christ (Isaiah 9:6), the 1948 declaration of the Nation of Israel (Luke 21:24) and the rise in this pre-apocalyptic decade of the Mark of the Beast, numbered 666 (Revelations 13:18).

These preachers – who, I must emphasise, are sincere though gravely misguided – argue that the biblical derivation of the values of the alphabet (a=6, b=12, c=18, d=24, e=30 etc) translates the words 'Computer' and 'Mark of Beast' into 666. This had led them to believe that the Beast was a computer owned by US diplomat Henry Kissinger, whose name also totals 666.

However, Daniel 7:8 reveals that the Beast shall rise in Europe, hence the preachers' recent move here after they chillingly discovered that your name, Gerry Adams, totals the dread 666 – as also, incredibly, does that of your political arch-enemy Ian Paisley.

Coincidence? Surely so. Yet these devout – and sincere – preachers remain convinced otherwise. I have promised to meet them again, either publicly or privately, to debate their theology. Perhaps you, as someone indirectly involved, could provide me with any advice on how best to demonstrate that what they are preaching is unfounded fundamentalist nonsense.

Yours sincerely,

John Mackay

Mr John Mackay

Dr. Ian Paisley, MP, MEP
Ravenshill Road,
Belfast,
Northern Ireland

Salem Court
Maxwell Road
Dublin 6

23 Feb 1993

Dear Dr. Paisley,

I am writing as a devout Christian with a spiritual problem which indirectly concerns you, and on which I hope you can give me some help and advice. I have in recent weeks met a group of inspirational American street preachers called the Society for the Negation of the Power of the Beast. They have explained to me the three major biblical prophetic fulfilments of this age - the birth of the One Lord and Saviour Jesus Christ (Isaiah 9:6), the 1948 declaration of the Nation of Israel (Luke 21:24) and the rise in this pre-apocalyptic decade of the Mark of the Beast, numbered 666 (Revelations 13:18).

These preachers - who, I must emphasise, are sincere though gravely misguided - argue that the biblical derivation of the values of the alphabet (a=6, b=12, c=18, d=24, e=30 etc) translates the words 'Computer' and 'Mark of Beast' into 666. This had led them to believe that the Beast was a computer owned by US diplomat Henry Kissinger, whose name also totals 666.

However, Daniel 7:8 reveals that the Beast shall rise in Europe, hence the preachers' recent move here after they chillingly discovered that your name, Ian Paisley, totals the dread 666 - as also, incredibly, does that of your political arch-enemy Gerry Adams.

Coincidence? Surely so. Yet these devout - and sincere - preachers remain convinced otherwise. I have promised to meet them again, either publicly or privately, to debate their theology. Perhaps you, as someone indirectly involved, could provide me with any advice on how best to demonstrate that what they are preaching is unfounded fundamentalist nonsense.

Yours sincerely,

John Mackay

Mr John Mackay

Salem Court
Maxwell Road
Dublin 6

30 July 1993

Mr & Mr Lever
Lever Brothers Ltd
3 St James Road
Kingston Upon Thames
Surrey KT1 29A
England

Dear Mr & Mr Lever,

I write regarding your Surf TV ad with Glenroe star Mary "Biddy" McEvoy; you know the one - it ends with Biddy's ringing assurance that "Lever Brothers will give you your money back".

Well, I want my money back. And I'll be straight with you. In my opinion, your powder seems fine on tee-shirts and jeans and key-rings and plates, but HOPELESS on bicycle mud-guards and weak on frying pans, particularly after curried beans and burned sausages.

I enclose the remains of the Surf, together with a stamped addressed envelope for the return of my money.

Yours sincerely,

John Mackay

Mr John Mackay

Our ref:

Your ref: BC/PG

Date:

23 August 1993

Lever Brothers (Ireland) Ltd.
Belgard Industrial Estate,
Belgard Road,
Tallaght, Dublin 24.
Telephone 527222.
Telex 91105.
Fax 527137

Mr John Mackay

Salem Court
Maxwell Road
Dublin 6

Dear Mr Mackay,

Thank you for your letter from which we were sorry to learn of your disappointment with our product, Surf.

Surf has been marketed for years as an excellent value for money brand, cleaning clothes effectively, even at low temperatures.

From the nature of your interesting letter we would like to stress that the product is suitable for cleaning garments. The alternative surfaces you describe as being inadequately cleaned, such as bicycle mud-guards and frying pans, are not generally recommended as being best cleaned with Surf. More suitable products for these purposes would include Quix Washing Up Liquid or even Jif Cream Cleaner for bicycle mud guards.

We hope this information has been of use to you and as a gesture of our goodwill we would be delighted if you would accept the enclosed vouchers to try some products which may be more suitable for the surfaces you described.

Thank you for contacting our firm.

Yours sincerely

Brona Cullen
CONSUMER ADVISORY SERVICE

Enc: Vouchers

Jif

TO THE CUSTOMER
This voucher entitles you to a Free Bottle
of Jif 500 ml. (up to the value of £1.20).

Domestos

Multi Surface Cleaner 500 ml.

FREE VOUCHER worth £1.40

TO THE CUSTOMER
This voucher entitles
of Domestos Multi
ml. (up to the value

TO THE TRADER
Lever Bros. (Irl.) Lte
Dublin 6, will redeem
of Domestos Multi S
ml. (up to the value o
item. Valid only in the

Salem Court
Maxwell Road
Dublin 6

9 March 1993

"Big" Jack Charlton,
Irish Team Manager,
c/o Football Association of Ireland,
80 Merrion Square,
Dublin 2

Dear "Big" Jack,

Wah-halk on, wah-halk on, with hope, in your heart, and you'll neh, veh-her walk, ah-ha-lone, you'll neh, veh-her walk, ah-ha-lone! Thanks to you this footballing anthem has finally made the transition from Tyneside and Wembley to the pleasant green turf of Lansdowne. You, "Big" Jack, have made the difference.

I followed your career at Leeds where you put the fear of Norman Hunter into opponents listed in your infamous black book of people to be "got". Not a pretty sight, and indeed behaviour which would probably have seen you share a cell with the Kray twins had you done so on the streets, but unarguably effective in a footballing sense - and a perfect foil to the flair of Eddie Gray, Peter Lorimer and "Gilesy".

Your no-nonsense style has since permeated your various management moves; America here we come, and I intend to be there. I am sure that you have, as they say, "inside info" on such logistics as venues and tickets etc. You and I are both straight-talking men, and know that the ethics of such fiscally-related arrangements are a different kettle of balls to the purity of the game on the field.

Where will we be playing? The name of the city will do. That way I can ensure sufficient surplus tickets and hotel accommodation for my good self to "pass on" at a legitimate profit to friends who will also be travelling.

Yours sincerely,

John Mackay

Mr John Mackay

PS I enclose a token £5 towards processing this application - boot it in the direction of whatever footballing or fishing expenditure you feel most appropriate!

THE FOOTBALL ASSOCIATION OF IRELAND

CUMANN PEILE NA hÉIREANN
FOUNDED 1921

80 Merrion Square, Dublin 2

WITH COMPLIMENTS

No further information until we qualify.

FIFA WORLD CUP GAME SCHEDULE

USA 19

17 June - 17 July 1994

WorldCupUSA94™

1991 WC 94 733

FIRST STAGE

		1 Friday 17 June	2 Saturday 18 June	3 Sunday 19 June	4 Monday 20 June	5 Tuesday 21 June	6 Wednesday 22 June	7 Thursday 23 June	8 Friday 24 June	9 Saturday 25 June	10 Sunday 26 June	11 Monday 27 June	12 Tuesday 28 June
	Los Angeles Stadium Rose Bowl		A3 v A4	B3 v B4			A1 v A3						
A	**San Francisco** Stadium Stanford				B1 v B2				B1 v B3	A1 v A4			
B	**Detroit** Stadium Pontiac Silverdome		A1 v A2				A4 v A2	B4 v B2		A2 v A3			B2 v B3 / B1 v B4
	Chicago Stadium Soldier Field		C1 v C2			C1 v C3							
C	**Boston** Stadium Foxboro									D4 v D2	C2 v C3		
D	**Dallas** Stadium Cotton Bowl		C3 v C4			D1 v D2 / D3 v D4	C4 v C2		D1 v D3				
	New York/ New Jersey Stadium Giants		E1 v E2				E1 v	F4 v			C1 v C4		

Salem Court
Maxwell Road
Dublin 6

The Holy Father
Vatican City
Rome, Italy

2 March 1993

Dear Holy Father,

In 1979 you told me you loved me across a crowded field in Galway, after an inspirational "warm-up" introduction by Bishop-without-portfolio, Eamonn Casey, the Brian Lenihan of your ecclesiastical Ard Fheis.

You told us to refrain from the sins of pre-marital flesh, support the church in all the anti-sexual referenda, and pass on to our children the time-honoured values with which we were indoctrinated.

Since then we have sunk ever deeper into a spiritual swamp governed by moral mutants and political pygmies - and surely the time has come for men of the cloth to stop playing doctors and nurses. The Faith of our Fathers has been disgraced, blasphemy is the oral currency, the fallen angel Beelzebub rushes in to fill the vacuum.

As you know, the Angelus bells must, by divine and secular law in Ireland, be played twice daily on our national radio and television. Recently, on the Pat Kenny radio show, no doubt because of sabotage by Godless communists, the Holy Bells failed to chime while the bells in hell went on going ting-a-ling-a-ling!

Holy Father, we are the butt of the jokes of every cheap lounge bar comedian and bus conducter. The "humour" ranges from the relatively harmless word-play of "what do you call a Bishop at Shannon Airport - A Papal leg-it" to an obscene visual joke where the teller asks why Bishops have double chins, then draws up an imaginary soutan to tuck under his chin while simulating the sin of Onan.

How do I react to such "jokes" and to the behaviour of my children, one of whom yesterday put a condom on one of the bishops in the family chess set?

Yours sincerely,

John Mackay

Mr John Mackay

PS I enclose a small donation which I would normally have given to one of your home-based staff.

SECRETARIAT OF STATE

FIRST SECTION · GENERAL AFFAIRS

No. 322.520   24 March 1993

Dear Mr Mackay,

    His Holiness Pope John Paul II has received
your letter, and he has directed me to reply in his
name.

    He wishes me to assure you that he is remem-
bering you and your family in his prayers.

    Your offering of five pounds is appreciated.

                              Yours sincerely,

                              Monsignor L. Sandri
                              Assessor

Mr John Mackay

Salem Court
Maxwell Road
Dublin 6

Salem Court
Maxwell Road
Dublin 6

18 May 1993

Mr Eugene Davy
Managing Director
Davy stockbrokers
49 Dawson Street
Dublin 2

Dear Mr Davy,

Like Ben Dunne after Florida, you emerged from a potential scarlet-face scenario with your reputation enhanced. You courageously chose to take the media flak full on when you were caught with your metaphorical pants around your fiscal ankles regarding the Greencore shares.

This, sir, is the opposite of a scandal - you put patriotism before profit when you purchased at a loss, with your own hard-earned money, the Greencore shares you had overpriced. Could Mr Ahern not have made clear to an economically illiterate public that here was a different spirit to the murky ghost of Greencore past?

And now you have waived your fees! Mr Davy, you are generous to a fault. You made a mistake in your sums (as my wife Dympna jokes, there are three kinds of stockbroker, those who can add and those who can't!) - but you are surely entitled to make good your error and restart the race.

I for one am impressed by your integrity, and I would like to avail of your services. Though I am currently not overtly wealthy, I am about to come into a pot of cash when my aged aunt crosses the road later this year. Mr Davy, I strongly suspect that I am talking middle to high six figures here, and I will need top advice on investing it.

What is the "market" like at present? Are we talking shares, houses, paintings, businesses, off-shore accounts? And how do you fit in fee-wise? Please let me know - I enclose five pounds for yourself to cover the administrative cost of processing this enquiry.

Yours sincerely,

John Mackay

Mr John Mackay

DAVY

PERSONAL INVESTMENT

Davy House
49 Dawson Street Dublin 2 Ireland
Telephone 6797788
Telex 93968 Fax 6796340

25th May 1993

John Mackay Esq.,

Salem Court,
Maxwell Road,
Dublin 6.

Dear Mr. Mackay,

Your letter to Eugene Davy of 18th May has been passed over to me. Mr. Davy has actually retired from the firm of which he was a founding partner, just over two years ago. However, we do appreciate your thoughtful comments at this particularly difficult time for our company.

Perhaps more importantly, we are confident that we will be able to put this set back behind us in the very near future, and look forward to resuming our normal low profile approach to generating good returns for our investment clients.

In this connection, I am pleased to enclose a copy of our *Investment Management Account* brochure, which will give you some idea of the scope of the services available here.

I also enclose some recent publications, which you may find helpful and of interest.

Working with Joseph Davy, Eugene Davy's son, I specialise in the management of private client portfolios, and I would be very pleased to meet with you to discuss these issues.

Finally, I am returning your postal order, since there are no costs involved in any consultations with this firm.

Thank you again for your good wishes.

Yours sincerely,

PETER KEANE

Encls./

Salem Court
Maxwell Road
Dublin 6

17 Feb 1993

John Bruton TD
Leader, Fine Gael
Leinster House

Dear Mr Bruton,

They say you have talked down both the pound and Fine Gael, but I have been in business and I fully support both your straight-talking rebuff of the Socialist Spring and your courageous call to devalue our currency. I was also enthralled by your recent ard-fheis speech which combined exciting new ideas on job creation with the traditional reactionary law and order policies this country so badly needs.

I have never been involved in politics, as to be honest I don't trust any of you but, having recently returned to Ireland, your reality-driven straight talking has given me food for thought. On reflection, it is not politicians but Fianna Fail who have caused my lapse of confidence in the political process.

Jobs - you are right - is the issue. Jobs and law and order. And people (every person counts). Would it be worth considering a people-based national security employment anti-crime policy, much like a full-time neighbourhood watch with access to legally-held weapons and payment for those involved, and with greater powers of enforcing citizen's arrests, obviously in consultation with local Gardai, and maybe coordinated by your ex-justice man Noonan? Only a suggestion. Perhaps some of your people could bounce it around.

Do you really think it is practical for Fine Gael to form the next Government? If so, I may consider joining. Please send me details on other party policies etc. If they are to my liking, I would be delighted to participate in your "handlers" group to prepare for the next time around - I am a man of both means and ideas, which I have put to good use for many charities, and I would be happy to devote some of my time to such a worthy cause as returning Fine Gael to power.

Yours sincerely,

John Mackay

Mr John Mackay

PS Please find enclosed a small donation to help tide the party over its current appalling position in the opinion polls. Also, what arrangements should I make to contribute regularly to the party by standing order?

Ref. MP   19th February 1993

Mr John Mackay,

Salem Court,
Maxwell Road,
Dublin 6.

Dear Mr Mackay,

I write to acknowledge with sincere thanks receipt of your correspondence of encouragement and support dated 17th February with enclosed contribution to party funds.

I have forwarded a copy of your letter and your donation to Fine Gael Headquarters, and requested that policy documents on various issues be forwarded to you for your information, and to arrange a standing order to enable you to contribute regularly to the Party.

This gesture is very much appreciated.

With kind regards

Yours sincerely,

JOHN BRUTON, TD
Leader, Fine Gael

FINE GAEL

Fine Gael National Headquarters, 51 Upper Mount Street, Dublin 2.
Tel: (01) 761573/611863. Fax: (01) 609168.

Ref: ID/EG

Mr. John Mackay,

Salem Court,
Maxwell Road,
Dublin 6.

24th February, 1993

Dear Mr. Mackay,

A copy of your recent letter to the Party Leader has been forwarded to me together with your kind donation to Party funds. I enclose some policy documents which may be of interest to you and I also enclose as requested a ticket for our national fundraising scheme (Funding Democracy) which can be paid by direct debit of £5.00 per month. Please complete and detach the portion of the ticket with the details of your Bank Account etc. and return it to me.

We greatly appreciate your support.

Kind regards,

Yours sincerely,

E. Gorman

P.P. IVAN DOHERTY
GENERAL SECRETARY

Donal Carey, T.D.,
Chairperson National
Executive

Encl.

Mr Noel Kennedy
Managing Director
Bus Eireann
Head Office
Broadstone
Dublin 7

Salem Court
Maxwell Road
Dublin 6

25 May 1993

Dear Mr Kennedy

I am currently in negotiations with RTE and the Dublin City Manager regarding a project with which I expect you will also wish to associate Bus Eireann. I know that joint ventures are the current fashion for semi-State companies, so locking yourselves in with a "sunrise" industry with a potential for megabucks should be right up Bus Eireann's alley!

Here's the plan: StarTour Eireann Ltd. Having recently returned from California where I took a tour of the stars' homes in Hollywood, I believe Dublin is ripe for the star tour plucking.

All you have to do is provide a luxury coach which meets our exacting specifications. After much consideration, I believe we should provide the driver as your lot seem prone to Luddite tendencies and industrial mayhem. I'm sure you agree.

The coach should seat a mimimum of 30 people with toilet facilities and be wired for video and public address facilities - we will want to show clips of the stars in action as we approach their homes.

Please oblige at your earliest convenience with a realistic opening bid. Also, is it possible to have a coach where the toilet may be used even when it is parked?

Yours sincerely,

John Mackay

Mr John Mackay

PS I hope you sort out those strikers before they wreck the country. I once heard a joke that went something like this - Dublin busman: "I see the daffodils are out". His colleague: "Will that affect us?" Feel free to use this joke at meetings with union "representatives"!

BUS EIREANN

PAUL DELEMERE

SALES EXECUTIVE

BUSÁRUS,
STORE ST., DUBLIN 1.
TEL: (01) 7032575
MOBILE (088) 592686
FAX: (01) 734534

Salem Court
Maxwell Road
Dublin 6

Mr Noel Kennedy
Managing Director   11 June 1993
Bus Eireann
Head Office
Broadstone
Dublin 7

Dear Mr Kennedy,

When I wrote to you on 25 May last, I expected to hear from the organ
grinder. What did I get? One of your sales monkeys calling personally
to my door, and leaving a note and a card through my letterbox.

Noel, I think this foot in the door merchant, ruthlessly efficient
though he clearly is, could be the first banana skin in what I had
hoped would be a one-to-one professional top-man-to-top-man interface
situation. I have always cut out the middle man; this is the difference
between public and private enterprise.

Please write to me with a realistic opening bid for a thrice-weekly
driver-suppliable thirty-punter rubbernecker-transporter or I fear that
StarTour Eireann will have to go elsewhere.

Yours sincerely,

John Mackay

Mr John Mackay

BROADSTONE
DUBLIN 7

TELEPHONE: (01) 302222
FAX: (01) 309377

REFER ENQUIRIES TO
EXTENSION

OUR REFERENCE   YOUR REFERENCE   6 July 1993 DATE

Mr. John Mackay,

Salem Court,
Maxwell Road,
Dublin 6.

Dear Mr. Mackay,

I refer to your letter dated 11th June 1993 and regret that any offence may have been caused by the personal call to you by our Sales Executive.

As you will appreciate, where there is a need for further details to be obtained or clarified, our normal course of action is to ask our Sales Executive for the area concerned to make a personal call.

In relation to your proposed tour I regret that we are not in a position to quote for your requirements at the moment as we do not have a vehicle in our fleet which would meet your specific needs.

I would like to thank you for your interest and wish you every success with your venture.

Yours sincerely,

N. Kennedy.

N. KENNEDY
Managing Director

BUS ÉIREANN — IRISH BUS — REGISTERED OFFICE: BROADSTONE DUBLIN 7
REGISTERED IN IRELAND NO. 119570

A SUBSIDIARY OF
CÓRAS IOMPAIR ÉIREANN

Salem Court
Maxwell Road
Dublin 6

10 August 1993

Chris de Burgh
Dalkey
County Dublin

Dear Chris,

Like many other Travelling Spacemen, I Paid the Ferryman when your Spanish Train came to Thurles for Féile '93! However, you crossed the Borderline with your Patricia The Stripper strip show. You were clearly High on Emotion as you helped your co-star Jaynene to undress, and I was Waiting For The Hurricane of protest that would bring down the Satin Green Shutters on your show.

Come on, Chris! It's one thing for the Golden Horde to be ordered off stage for offensive language by the Gardai. They have an excuse – Simon Carmody was educated by the Christian Brothers. I can even tolerate the maggot-munching Jim Rose Circus freaks lifting weights using anatomically unsuitable body parts.

But you, Chris, have always been different: an oasis of musical sanity amidst multiple sandstorms of moral vulgarity. Yet here you were, assisting a voluptuous young suspender-clad lady to sensuously wriggle out of her clothing as she tantalisingly teased you with a provocative hip-swaying "dance".

This, Chris, is an abuse of women, even if Jaynene was clearly consenting. Consent, as you know, is only an acceptable justification for behaviour if we agree with the behaviour.

However, since everyone enjoyed it, I will overlook the lapse if you will send me a signed photo of yourself and Jaynene on stage. I enclose £5 to cover any postage and administrative costs; if there's anything left over, give it to the taxman (but not the Ferryman!).

Yours sincerely,

John Mackay

Mr John Mackay

IDA IRELAND

INDUSTRIAL DEVELOPMENT
AUTHORITY OF IRELAND

WILTON PARK HOUSE
WILTON PLACE
DUBLIN 2   IRELAND
TELEPHONE (01) 686633
688444 602244
FACSIMILE (01) 603703
TELEX 93431

Mr John Mackey

Salem Court
Maxwell Road
Dublin 6

23 March 1993

Dear Mr Mackey

Further to your recent correspondence with Kieran McGowan, I would like to meet with you to discuss your proposal. As I do not have a telephone number for you, perhaps you could call me and we could set up a meeting.

Yours sincerely

Colm MacFhionnlaoich
Manager
Small Business Division

Mr Colm MacFhionnlaoich
Manager, Small Business Division
IDA
Wilton Park House
Wilton Place
Dublin 2

Salem Court
Maxwell Road
Dublin 6

25 May 1993

Dear Mr MacFhionnlaoich,

My apologies for the delay in responding to yours of 23 March; I have
been out of the country involving myself in further market research on
the dogbowl project. Countries visited: <u>Four</u> (4). Countries with
commercial availability of dogfood bowls modelled as plexiglass dinner
plates: <u>Zero</u> (0).

Perhaps we should be looking at the possibility of an export-led
marketing drive? Or maybe start small at home and expand? Whichever, I
will be delighted to meet with you. To maximise the benefit extractable
from your valuable time, I'll do the following advance leg-work:

1. Test-feed various size prototypes with various size dogs (Economy
Size for the Chihuahua; Master Dish for the Great Dane etc);
2. Bounce around the idea of "add-on" products (perhaps a joint
venture with Beleek or Arklow Pottery, for the discerning dog);
3. Bounce around the idea of "novelty" products (portable dogbowl
with attachment for muzzle with air vents for Rottweillers etc).

I hope you will agree that we must walk before we can bark. Our main
focus must remain on the original product - the "add-ons" may be fun,
but it's hard work that pays the rent.

I have also commissioned a sample print advert (enclosed) which I hope
captures the flavour of the "Unique Selling Point" of the proposed
product. Please let me know where I could find current samples of trade
or media adverts for existing dogbowls, here or abroad.

Please also either send me what details you can on the current dogbowl
(and related products) market in Ireland, or else point me in the right
direction and I'll sniff them out myself.

Yours sincerely,

John Mackay

Mr John Mackay

PS I have let the Taoiseach know that you are now handling the IDA end
of the venture. I must stress that both he and I would wish that this
viability study be treated strictly on its commercial merits - please
feel free to shout "stop!" if the market dictates. Bottom line.

Salem Court
Maxwell Road
Dublin 6

25 May 1993

SAMPLE DRAFT DESIGN FOR
PRINT ADVERT HIGHLIGHTING
UNIQUE SELLING POINT
OF IRISH-MANUFACTURED
DOGFOOD BOWLS MODELLED AS
PLEXIGLASS DINNER PLATES

SUBMITTED TO MR COLM MAC FHIONNLAOICH,
MANAGER, SMALL BUSINESS DIVISION, IDA,
FOR USE IN COMMERCIAL VIABILITY ENQUIRY
INSTIGATED BY AN TAOISEACH, MR ALBERT REYNOLDS TD

WILTON PARK HOUSE
WILTON PLACE
DUBLIN 2 IRELAND
TELEPHONE (01) 686633
688444 602244
FACSIMILE (01) 603703
TELEX 93431

Mr John MacKay

Salem Court
Maxwell Road
Dublin 6

2 June 1993

Dear Mr MacKay

Thank you for your recent letter. I am delighted to see work continuing on the idea. I would be pleased to meet with you at your convenience. As I do not have a telephone number for you could you call me to set up a meeting. It is important, if you are seeking grant aid for a feasibility study, to talk to us and get grant approval before spending any money which might be claimed under a feasibility study grant.

In regard to your queries on the current size of the Irish market you should contact An Bord Trachtala and they may be able to help, otherwise, it will be a question of talking to distributors and agents or relevant trade bodies to ascertain the figures.

In relation to trade and media adverts, perhaps the library in An Bord Trachtala would have magazines carrying suitable advertisements.

Once again, please contact me as soon as possible to arrange a meeting.

Yours sincerely

Colm MacFhionnlaoich
Manager
Small Business Division

Maire Geoghegan Quinn TD
Minister for Justice
Department of Justice
Stephens Green

Salem Court
Maxwell Road
Dublin 6

18 May 1993

Dear Ms Geoghegan Quinn,

You are our Queen Canute of the Crime Waves, as we drown in a tide of muggers and thugs - and your courage in speaking out against the sexist discrimination that is rife in Fianna Fail marks you out as a woman of action with a future.

I used to live in Galway - my family still do, and you always get their number 1 - and we have followed your political career with Galwegian pride since you overtook the talented Countess Markievicz as the first woman Cabinet Minister since the foundation of the State.

Well done on your crack-down on teenagers roaming freely through O'Connell Street without good reason. Those of a civil libertarian bent will no doubt whinge that you are infringing some alleged "right" or other. Ignore them, Maire - without law, there is no order.

I was also relieved to see the dropping of the scandalous charges against the High Court Judge who should never have been asked to accompany the Gardai to their station for seeking an after-hours drink in the Shelbourne. Judges are not ordinary citizens; they are the very foundation of law and order. They deserve an after-hours tipple after a stressful day locking up the very people your latest bill is designed to harrass.

So well done, Maire; you have started your tenure with style. I can assure you that you have certainly retained my family's votes back in Galway. Would it help to bring back public floggings? My wife Dympa and I were impressed at its effectiveness in the Isle of Man, and we would appreciate the benefit of your opinion on importing the measure.

Yours faithfully,

John Mackay

Mr John Mackay

PS I enclose a token donation towards your next election campaign, as a Justice Minister prepared to protect law and order.

OIFIG AN AIRE DLÍ AGUS CIRT
(OFFICE OF THE MINISTER FOR JUSTICE)
BAILE ÁTHA CLIATH
(DUBLIN)

28 May, 1993.

Dear Mr. Mackay,

I write to acknowledge receipt of your letter dated 18 May, 1993 which
I will bring to the Minister's attention.

Yours sincerely,

J. Adwyn

Private Secretary

Salem Court
Maxwell Road
Dublin 6

10 August 1993

Maire Geoghegan Quinn
Minister for Justice
Department of Justice
Stephens Green

Dear Ms Geoghegan Quinn,

I wrote to you on 18 May, asking your opinion on the selective public
flogging of criminals, and enclosing £5 for your next campaign.
Your private secretary responded to the effect that my letter would
be brought to your attention, but I have yet to receive your reply.
I will soon be visiting my family in Galway - who have always voted
for you - and I would love to have your reply to show them!

Yours sincerely,

John Mackay

Mr John Mackay

17 September, 1993.

Dear Mr. Mackay,

I am directed by the Minister for Justice Mrs. Máire Geoghegan-Quinn, T.D., to refer to your recent letter regarding selective public flogging of criminals.

The Minister has noted with interest the contents of your letter and has referred it to the Garda Commissioner for his attention.

The Minister has asked me to acknowledge receipt of your donation towards the Fianna Fáil Party.

Yours sincerely,

Private Secretary

Mr John Mackay

Salem Court
Maxwell Road
Dublin 6

Salem Court
Maxwell Road
Dublin 6

24 September 1993

The Commissioner
Gardai Siochana
Phoenix Park
Dublin 8

Dear Commissioner Culligan,

When I wrote to you last June, you were good enough to put me right on the non-existance of the Irish Burglars Association.

I have since been in touch with Maire Geoghegan Quinn proposing the selective public flogging of criminals - a natural follow-on to Bishop Comiskey's recent sensible endorsement of ear-cuffing and wooden-spooning of children.

As I know that Maire has referred the proposal to you, I want to stress that the word "selective" should not be interpreted too restrictively.

What I had in mind was a scale of intensity that allows most criminals to be flogged, with perhaps a short flogging at home being adequate for first offences, and a public stocks-type flogging reserved for serious rowdies and repeat undesirables.

I hope that this clarification will be useful in your deliberations on the matter.

Yours sincerely,

John Mackay

Mr John Mackay

AN GARDA SIOCHANA

Any reply to this communication should be
addressed to:

Commissioner,
Garda Síochána,
Phoenix Park,
Dublin 8.

and the following number quoted:

OIFIG AN CHOIMISINEARA,

BAILE ÁTHA CLIATH.

P.S. 216/93

29th September 1993

Mr. John Mackay,

Salem Court,
Maxwell Road,
Dublin 6.

Dear Mr. Mackay,

I am directed by the Commissioner to refer to your letter of 24th September 1993.

You will, no doubt, be aware that the Garda Siochana implements criminal law enacted by the legislature, and the judiciary apportion punishment in accordance with law. It is, therefore, inappropriate for the Garda Siochana to comment on any proposal which does not necessitate Garda involvement.

Yours sincerely,

JOHN V. KENNEDY
SUPERINTENDENT
PRIVATE SECRETARY
TO COMMISSIONER

Salem Court
Maxwell Road
Dublin 6

5 October 1993

Maire Geoghegan Quinn TD
Minister for Justice
Department of Justice
Stephens Green

Dear Ms Geoghegan Quinn,

I wrote to you some months ago regarding the public chastisement of bad articles and ne'er-do-wells, and you sensibly referred my proposal to the Garda Commissioner.

I have just received the Commissioner's kick to touch. It displays little enthusiasm for Garda involvement in flogging, and bounces the ball and chain firmly back onto your level playing field. Minister, you may well choose to take him aside and put him right on this one.

I assume he is one of us.

If the difficulty lies in recruiting an administrator to carry out the floggings, may I volunteer my services - I get so angry watching Crime Watch that Dympna already calls me John Pierrepoint Mackay!

You will be glad to hear that I have faxed copies of your letter to my family in Galway, who are greatly impressed by your efficient and practical response to a suggestion from an ordinary citizen.

Yours sincerely,

John Mackay

Mr John Mackay

PS Here's another fiver for your next election campaign fund!

OIFIG AN AIRE DLÍ AGUS CIRT
(OFFICE OF THE MINISTER FOR JUSTICE)
BAILE ÁTHA CLIATH
(DUBLIN)

11 October, 1993.

Dear Mr. Mackay,

I am directed by the Minister for Justice, Mrs. Máire Geoghegan-Quinn, T.D., to refer further to your recent letter.

The Minister has asked me to say that she has noted your comments and that the donation enclosed with your letter has been forwarded to Fianna Fáil Party Headquarters.

Yours sincerely,

J. Odwyer
Private Secretary

Mr John Mackay

Salem Court
Maxwell Road
Dublin 6

Mr Dermot Morgan
Cue Productions
7 Bridge Street
Ringsend
Dublin 4

Salem Court
Maxwell Road
Dublin 6

24 September 1993

Dear Mr Morgan,

My wife Dympna and her mother Maisie share a birthday in January (who says lightning doesn't strike in the same place twice! Ho ho!) and I am thinking of organising a bit of a surprise party at home for them. Perhaps foolishly, I have occasionally spoofed to Dympna, my son, Toby, and daughter, Susie, that I met you, so if you were to be my guest at the party it would be a thrill for all of us.

We will be clearing a place in the living room for you to do your act and Toby has agreed to work the standard lamp and record player for you as well as attending to other chores usually undertaken by a stage manager. Being "an old pal of Jay McKay", you can join us for the meal and, before the date, I will fill you in on the "shared experiences" I have told my family about, so we can appear to have a bond beyond "boss and hired help."

I know you don't come cheap, and have budgeted for a hefty three-figure fee. No one there except me and you will know you are being paid for the "gig". Let me know your requirements — I can pick you up in the jalopy, if you don't want to take a taxi — and I enclose £5 to cover any expenses involved at this stage.

Yours sincerely,

John Mackay

Mr John Mackay

PS Just one further favour: I would appreciate it if you could drop your satirical Eamon Dunphy ditty "Release The Little Bollox in D Wing". Maisie had a run-in with the Road Traffic Acts some years ago and incontinence became a serious inconvenience when you sang it on the Late Late Show recently.

PPS Dermot, positively NO mother-in-law jokes!

CUE PRODUCTIONS LTD ▶▶▶

7 Bridge Street, Ringsend, Dublin 4.
Telephone 602275.

18th October, 1993.

Mr. John MacKay,

Salem Court,
Maxwell Road,
Dublin 6.

Dear John,

Sincere apologies for not writing back to you sooner re. Dermot Morgan. We have been very busy touring and this is my first opportunity I have had to get back to you.

I am delighted to hear Dympna and Maisie share the same birthday and Dermot appreciates the kind invitation to the party. However, Dermot will be in Switzerland and busy touring in Ireland throughout January so unfortunately will not be able to attend.

In the meantime, I will send you back your £5 which you should find enclosed with this letter.

Yours sincerely,

Sonya Fildes

Sonya Fildes
PA to Dermot Morgan

Salem Court
Maxwell Road
Dublin 6

Desmond O'Malley TD
Leader Progressive Democrats
Leinster House

17 Feb 1993

Dear Mr O'Malley,

Congratulations on almost doubling your representation in the Dail – despite polling less votes than last time. The mysteries of PR indeed! Congratulations also on getting two of your people into the Senate, from whence to more effectively campaign for its abolition.

It was also heartening to hear you during the Taoiseach vote place the leftist rabble led by Spring and de Rossa firmly in the same political dustbin reserved for Neil Kinnock by the British electorate. Though the bumbling Bruton may have sent Spring scuttling into the arms of Albert, there is hope left for Ireland in your forthright fearlessness.

I listened to your recent ard-fheis speech. Excellent, though at times you tended to stray – I am sure unintentionally – down the blind alley of promoting the jaded and failed socialist values now discredited throughout Europe. I refer to your preponderance of references to "Irish society" rather than "Irish business" when, without Irish business, Irish society simply could not exist. Money makes the world go round, world go round etc.

I realise some throwing of such "caring" shapes was helpful in pacifying your ideologically vacant government "partners" of the time. However, now that you are free to say what you mean, please remember (as Michael McDowell has made clear) that the Progressive Democrats must be right-wing or redundant. Perhaps you might consider asking Sunday Business Post economist Mary Ellen Synon to join your "handlers" group?

I am writing to offer my own advice and services to your Party. I am of means, self-made, up to now politically uninvolved. I understand economics and business, and I can spot leftist rhetoric with my ears shut. For a nominal fee plus appropriate expenses, I would be delighted to participate in your "handlers" group.

Please find enclosed a token donation to the Party by way of indicating my commitment to such values. Also, what arrangements should I make to contribute regularly to the party by standing order?

Yours sincerely,

John Mackay

Mr John Mackay

PS You might consider settling your differences with the Goodman lads who, despite whatever white lies they may be alleged to have told to unimportant people, were actively involved in creating the profits and jobs we all want in this country. Bottom line.

18th February 1993

Mr John Mackay

Salem Court
Maxwell Road
Dublin 6

Dear Mr Mackay

Thank you for your letter of 17th February, 1993 enclosing a
Postal Order for £5.00 in favour of the Progressive Democrats
which we are lodging to our General Election Campaign fund. If
you wish to make any further contributions to the Party they
would of course be very welcome. I am sending a copy of your
letter to our General Secretary, Michael Parker.

Best wishes.

Yours sincerely

DESMOND O'MALLEY T.D.
Leader of the Progressive Democrats

Salem Court
Maxwell Road
Dublin 6

25 May 1993

Desmond O'Malley TD
Leader, Progressive Democrats
Leinster House

Dear Mr O'Malley,

I don't want to be telling tales out of school, but there are serious administrative problems within your Party.

I wrote to you on 17 Feb offering to participate in your "handlers" group, and enclosing a token £5 donation to bolster the Party coffers. Your response was both efficient (by return post) and courteous, and you sent the matter "down the line" to a Mr Parker.

To date - fully THREE MONTHS later - I have heard NOTHING from this man. Zero. Zilch. Mr O'Malley, the letterbox is bare. This does not augur well; how, I may ask, would Mr Culliton react to such laxity?

In the circumstances, I have no option but to request the immediate return of my money unless I hear from Mr Parker THIS WEEK outlining how I can contribute to the work of the Party's "Think Tank".

I am sorry to be so blunt about this, you're a good man yourself, Mr O'Malley, but that's the way life is - you deliver or you're dead in the water.

Yours sincerely,

John Mackay

John Mackay

PS I was glad to see you slam that nonsense about your brother-in-law buying your wife a new frock - do these "political commentators" live in the real world at all, or what?

Michael McDowell TD
Leinster House

Salem Court
Maxwell Road
Dublin 6

2 July 1993

Dear Mr McDowell,

I understand that you have some familiarity with the law. I write to ask advice on recovering a £5 donation which I made to your party leader, Mr Desmond O'Malley, chronologically thusly:

(1) 17 Feb 1993: On returning home after a spell overseas doing this and that, I sent Mr O'Malley £5 and offered my services as a political "handler". He responded to the effect that he was sending my letter "down the line" to a Mr Parker.

(2) 25 May 1993: THREE MONTHS LATER, on hearing NOTHING further, I wrote to Mr O'Malley in the following explicit terms: "I have no option but to request the immediate return of my money unless I hear from Mr Parker THIS WEEK outlining how I can contribute to the work of the Party's Think Tank".

(3) Today: OVER FOUR MONTHS LATER, no response from Mr O'Malley, Mr Parker or ANYONE connected with the Party - AND the stamped addressed envelope I enclosed has simply been pocketed.

Mr McDowell, what is happening here? Does Mr Parker exist? Is his typewriter broken? Does the Party routinely "fob off" ordinary people such as I? I am angry, Mr McDowell, though I know that you, as a pillar of fiscal integrity and ideological intellect, are not and never would be party to such peurile political practice.

I am sure you will agree that I have been deprived of my money in questionable legal circumstances, and that I am entitled to immediate recovery of same, together with compensation of appropriate though not punitive consequence, either through voluntary fiscal retribution or by plodding the sad path of due process.

I would appreciate your advice in the matter.

Yours sincerely,

John Mackay

Mr John Mackay

PS I am very impressed with the Party's recent Dail performance. Well done. However, in light of the above internal contretemps, it puts me in mind of a duck swimming - smooth and calm above the waterline, no end of flapping and fluster underneath!

PPS While I write to you as a TD, I acknowledge that this letter also impinges on your area of legal expertise; I therefore enclose £5 to cover the cost of processing this enquiry.

●Travelling by boat:
Maire Geoghegan-Qu...

...he asked. "Wi...
...ty Mouse Jim adopts ...
philosophical tone and talks about Pyrrhic victories,
the media concludes there is no story. But the day
Jim will say 'No, I am not having this,' then there is
real news and danger for the Government."

Frustrated PD 'handler' asks for fiver back

PD DEPUTY Michael McDowell recently received the following communication from a frustrated, would-be political handler for the party, with an address in Dublin 6.

Dear Michael,

I understand that you have some familiarity with the law. I write to ask advice on recovering a £5 donation which I made to your party leader, Mr Desmond O'Malley, chronologically thusly:

1. 17 Feb., 1993: On returning home after a spell overseas doing this and that, I sent Mr O'Malley £5 and offered my services as a political "handler." He responded to the effect that he was sending my letter "down the line" to a Mr Parker.

2. 25 May, 1993: Three months later, on hearing nothing further, I wrote to Mr O'Malley in the following explicit terms: "I have no option but to request the immediate return of my money unless I hear from Mr Parker this week, outlining how I can contribute to the work of the party's Think Tank.

3. Today: Over four months later, no response from anyone connected with the party — and the stamped addressed envelope I enclosed has simply been pocketed. Mr McDowell, what is happening here? Does Mr Parker exist? Is his typewriter broken?

Does the party routinely "fob off" ordinary people such as I? I am angry, Mr McDowell, though I know that you, as a pillar of fiscal integrity and ideological intellect, are not and never would be, party to such puerile political practice.

I am sure you will agree that I have been deprived of my money in questionable legal circumstances, and that I am entitled to immediate recovery of same, together with com-

●Holding on to the fiver: Michael McDowell

pensation of appropriate, though not punitive, consequence, either through voluntary fiscal retribution or by plodding the sad path of due process.

I would appreciate your advice in the matter.

Yours sincerely,

John Mackay.

PS: I am very impressed with the party's recent Dail performance. Well done. However, in light of the above internal contretemps, it puts me in mind of a duck swimming — smooth and calm above the waterline, no end of flapping and fluster underneath.

PPS: While I write to you as a TD, I acknowledge that this letter also impinges on your area of legal expertise. I therefore enclose £5 to cover the cost of processing this enquiry.

Deputy McDowell is still trying to confirm the existence of Mr Mackay. Meanwhile, he is holding on to the £5!

●The main contende...

Will M be FG

FINE GAEL'S M...
is regarded as b...
back in contentio...
leadership stakes,...
non-scripted closin...
the Dail on the Aer...
plan on Wednesday ...

Government and Oppos...
that it was a masterpiece...
culminating in his putdo...
chief whip, Michael Ferr...
dared to interrupt the F...
claim he had no consci...

Sharp as a new pin,...
retorted: "At least y...
jobs in Clonmel bef...
arrived." This was a...
reference to the leak...
confidential details ...
plant for South Tippe...
allegedly led the comp...
reconsider its plans to ...

Despite Fine Gael's po...

Mary Harney TD
Leader, Progressive Democrats
Leinster House
Dublin 2

Salem Court
Maxwell Road
Dublin 6

20 October 1993

Dear Ms Harney,

Firstly, congratulations on your election as party leader.
Now, down to business (that's how it is at the top).
Dessie may not have told you, but his sudden resignation coincided with
a potential financial scandal involving himself, myself and a five pound
postal order which I sent him in February.
Michael McDowell may not have told you, but his reluctance to throw
his wig and gown into the ring for the top job coincided with his
involvement in this dispute - he pocketed a second fiver in July when
I asked him to intercede on my behalf.
Could you perhaps take them aside and mark their cards on this?
I'm a reasonable man, but my patience has its limits.

Yours sincerely,

John Mackay

Mr John Mackay

PS Here's another fiver

Salem Court
Maxwell Road
Dublin 6

3 June 1993

Mr Christy Kirwan
Chairman, FAS
FAS Head Office
Baggot Street
Dublin 2

Dear Mr Kirwan,

At last, the insidious feminist contamination of Irish thinking is openly challenged by a man in public life. You are so right; "all women will always be girls" and typing is not a skill - of course it isn't: I typed this letter myself!

For your courage, you will be pilloried by the politically correct, nagged by bitter women and bitched at by "new" men. But you, sir, can become the truth-bearing orthodox-challenging Gender Galileo of our age.

You have studied economics, organised Irish workers, served in Seanad Eireann; most importantly, you are a <u>MAN</u>. Say no more - or, in this instance, say <u>much</u> more!

I am writing a book titled "Irish Men Debate Irish Feminism - Wombs With A View Or Ovaries With Attitude?". It will be presented in a "for and against" format which, like society, will be suitably weighted to ensure that the right side wins.

I would be grateful if you would write the foreword to the book. About 800 words will do; the copy deadline is one months time and I will, of course, cut you in on the action for your participation.

Please also enclose a photo of your good self for the foreword page; I enclose £5 to cover the costs of same.

Yours sincerely,

John Mackay

Mr John Mackay

PS Is it true that you also run the Irish Boxing Association? If so, a photo of you wearing boxing gloves would convey an appropriately "masculine" image.

FÅS Foras Áiseanna Saothair
TRAINING & EMPLOYMENT AUTHORITY

14 June, 1993

27-33 Upper Baggot Street, Dublin 4, Ireland.
Telephone (01) 685777. Telex 93313 FÁS El. Fax (01) 682691.

Mr John Mackay

Salem Court
MAXWELL ROAD
Dublin 6

Dear Mr Mackay

I acknowledge receipt of your letter of June 3, last, concerning recent press coverage on remarks made by me, in 1984, during an appeal of a Labour Court recommendation.

I return herewith your Postal Order in the sum of Ir£5, uncashed, together with a copy of my Press Statement released earlier this month. I would advise that I do not intend to take any further action in this regard.

Yours sincerely

Chris Kirwan
CHAIRMAN

IRISH POSTAL ORDER — ORDÚ POIST
Head Office
Baile Átha Cliath
NOT NEGOTIABLE
0510235
£5.00

Foras Áiseanna Saothair
TRAINING & EMPLOYMENT AUTHORITY

PRESS STATEMENT

P.O. Box 456, 27-33 Upper Baggot Street, Dublin 4, Ireland.
Phone (01) 668 5777, Telex 93313 FAS EI, Fax (01) 668 2691.

FAS CHAIRMAN RESPONSE TO PRESS COMMENT

I refer to recent press coverage concerning remarks made by me in 1984 during an appeal of a Labour Court recommendation.

At the outset, I would like to state that these remarks were made, nine years ago, in the context of an industrial relations process and in the context of advocacy which this process requires. These remarks were a very small part of an overall submission to the Court and were never designed to cause upset or insult. They do not reflect my position.

The publication of these remarks nine years later in isolation could give an erroneous impression of my personal commitment to the promotion of equality in Ireland particularly equality within the labour force.

During my period as General Secretary of the largest trade union in the country, more women were appointed to frontline trade union positions than ever before. As President of the Irish Congress of Trade Unions, I led the negotiations for the Programme for Economic and Social Progress which included many elements designed to promote equality of opportunity. Similarly, while I was a Board member and Chairman of FAS, the organisation pioneered the introduction of Positive Action Programmes for Women. These Programmes have increased the number of women undertaking non-traditional training and employment programmes. Furthermore, the recent Report of the Second Commission on the Status of Women recommended that other educational and training bodies should introduce programmes on a similar basis to FAS.

I consider that my record in the trade union movement and more recently as Chairman of FAS gives ample evidence of my commitment.

Chris Kirwan
Chairman

Bishop Jeremiah Newman
Limerick

25 May 1993

Dear Bishop Newman,

My wife Dympna and I have just returned from an American holiday, where we heard from a former Limerick man of your run-in with the crazy cult leader David Koresh, late of Waco, Texas. Perhaps you could fill us in any missing pieces in the story.

We know that Mr Koresh spent some time in your Bishopric - an unwelcome side effect of the Shannon stopover - "recruiting" in Limerick and harvesting souls for his "cult". Dympna has also heard that he cut something of a dash on the burgeoning Limerick social scene, regularly proseltsying in "Durty Nellies", occasionally promulgating his heresy in Patrick Punch's fine public house.

He apparently attempted to join some of the better golf clubs, and there was dark talk of him cheating by dropping a substitute ball down the leg of his waterproof trousers when his own ball was lost in a Captain's Prize competition in the late '80s. Surely such heretical behaviour should have alerted the good burgers of your patch!

We believe he also had a run in with the departed Bishop Casey of Galway when it became apparent that he had set his sights on establishing Limerick as the epicentre of his devilish cult, and I was delighted to hear that you then used your considerable political "pull" to have him deported from Shannon with a couple of Cuban malcontents.

Again, well done, Your Grace. You have always been my favourite Bishop. Please let me have a photograph, signed, "To John and Dympna Mackay, not forgetting little Toby and Suzie, my dear, dear friends." I enclose £5 for the postage; please give any change to old Casey in Mexico.

Yours sincerely,

John Mackay

John Mackay

PHONE 061-315856

FAX 061-310186

31/5/93

IRISH POSTAL ORDER · ORDU P

0510235

£5.00

Diocesan Offices
66 O'Connell Street
Limerick

With Compliments

Bishop Newman is grateful for your concern but he knows nothing about the matter.

(Rev.) Liam O'Sullivan.

Salem Court
Maxwell Road
Dublin 6

3 June 1993

The Manager
Shelbourne Hotel
Stephens Green
Dublin 2

Dear Mr Moran,

I am expecting some relatives from the United States for a visit later this year and I am preparing a programme of entertainment to keep them amused during their stay in our fair city.

Could you please let me know the best time and night to visit the Horseshoe Bar to ensure that we catch the spectacle of the Barristers revealing intimate secrets and threatening each other?

Also, can you recommend the best seats from which to watch the judges demanding their after-hours drinks?

Finally, if I send you a photograph of myself and my wife Dympna in advance of the evening, could you arrange for your staff to greet us on familiar first-name terms? I'll tip appropriately!

Yours sincerely,

John Mackay

Mr John Mackay

The Shelbourne

St. Stephen's Green, Dublin 2, Ireland.
Telephone: 01-676 6471 Telex: 93653 Facsimile: 01-661 6006

PJM/ab

8th June, 1993

Mr John Mackay

Salem Court
Maxwell Road
Dublin 6

Dear Mr Mackay

Thank you for your letter of 3rd June.

While a great deal of planning goes into many aspects of our guests' enjoyment of The Shelbourne, the spirit of each evening rises spontaneously from our guests themselves and cannot be guaranteed to be quite as spectacular as you might perhaps have hoped.

However, I am sure you and your guests will find much to entertain you and, while I am afraid we would not be able to arrange to identify you with quite the familiarity you suggest, nevertheless, I am sure you will be welcomed with the same warmth and hospitality that we extend to all our guests.

I hope you enjoy your evening.

Yours sincerely

Peter J Moran
Resident Manager

FORTE GRAND

Forte Ireland Limited. A company registered in the Republic of Ireland under No 18441.
Registered office 27 St. Stephen's Green, Dublin 2, Ireland.
Directors: D Hearn Chairman (British) A Giannuzzi (Italian) A J Hearn (British)
P J Shortall Lt Col J E D Silcock P M Stephenson Sir John Swinson KB OBE (British)

Salem Court
Maxwell Road
Dublin 6

26 July 1993

Bertie Ahern TD
Minister for Finance
Department of Finance
Merrion Street
Dublin 2

Dear Mr Ahern,

That's it! I've had enough! I wrote to you FIVE MONTHS ago, with a £5 donation, seeking permission for my niece to include two anodyne anecdotes about your good self in her thesis. I wrote again TWO MONTHS ago politely reminding you that you had not replied.

Bertie, I'm not going for a hat-trick. I'm cashing in my chips, along with my Irish citizenship. My wife Dympna and I, along with our son Toby and daughter Suzie, plan to make a fresh start in a country where the money medicine man is more reliable – we're thinking of Nigeria.

John Mackay is something of a Shakespearean scholar (which is probably all Greek to you) and he lives by the philosophy "neither a borrower or a lender be". I have calculated that the Mackay family share of the National Debt runs to nearly £30,000, which we will pay before we leave. However, I do insist that our share of the Euro £8 billion be subtracted, along with the fiver I sent you in the dim distant past of February.

The sums work out roughly thusly:

National Debt (approximately)	IR£	25,000,000,000
Amount Owed per Person	IR£	7,200
Amount Owed by Mackay Family	IR£	28,800
Less Mackay Share of Euro £8b	IR£	9,200
Less £5 Sent in February	IR£	5
Balance Owed by Mackay Family	IR£	19,595

Please have one of your mandarins check the above sums (you'll find the figures change significantly if you adjust them in the same way as you adjusted the £8 billion) and invoice me accordingly.

I can only add that it is with deep regret that I leave the land of my forefolks – however, your laissez faire Ministerial attitude to a simple request, twice made, from an Irish citizen, leave me no choice. Farewell.

Yours sincerely,

John Mackay

Mr John Mackay

The Ambassador to Ireland
The Nigerian Embassy
56 Leeson Park
Dublin 6

Salem Court
Maxwell Road
Dublin 6

26 July 1993

Your Excellency,

As you may know, I sent some money to our Minister for Finance, Mr Bertie Ahern, on February 17 of this year, but received no satisfaction. I wrote to him again on May 18, and again received no reply.

You will appreciate that an individual facing such an uncaring bureaucracy must confront the reality that he is not wanted, and I have reluctantly decided to forego my Irish citizenship and seek to follow my fortunes elsewhere.

My wife Dympna has visited Lagos (where I understand Guinness have a brewery) and she tells me that the sun shines a lot there and everyone is happy. I hear you have recently taken a military government – unlike many "liberal" westerners, I have no objection to that. Indeed, perhaps the Irish Army should send an observer with a view to imposing greater discipline on Irish society.

Please send me the necessary forms for myself, my wife Dympna, my son Toby and my daughter Suzie to become Nigerian citizens. I enclose £5 to facilitate any administrative costs.

Yours sincerely,

John Mackay

Mr John Mackay

30th July 1993

Mr John Mackey

Salem court
Maxwell Road
Dublin 6

Dear John

I would like to thank you for forwarding towards the Fianna Fail
debt your kind donation.

With regard to the quotes unfortunately I cannot recall the
incident in question and there fore cannot verify them.
778
Best wishes.

Yours sincerely,

Bertie

Bertie Ahern, TD
Minister for Finance
cl/as

EMBASSY OF NIGERIA,

56 LEESON PARK,

DUBLIN, 6.

REPUBLIC OF IRELAND.

TELEPHONES 604366, 604051 AND 604092
TELS. & CABLES—NIGERIAN, DUBLIN
TELEX NO. 24163

Ref. No.

9th August, 1993.

Mr. J. Mackay,

Salem Court,
Maxwell Road,
Dublin, 6.

Dear Mr. J. Mackay,

    I am directed to refer to your letter of 26th July, 1993 and to thank you for your interest in Nigeria.

2.   On your quest for Nigerian Citizenship, however, I wish to inform you that you are required to have worked/lived in any part of the country for a minimum of 10 years, before putting up your initial application to the relevant authorities.

3.   We hereby also, return your enclosed £5.00 Postal Order.

                Yours sincerely,

                U. B. Okafor,
                for Ambassador.

Salem Court
Maxwell Road
Dublin 6

Mr Simon Corah
Managing Director
Saatchi and Saatchi Advertising
4 Clonskeagh Road
Dublin 14

28 June 1993

Dear Mr Corah,

No doubt your team is conceptually familiar with the Hollywood tourist trap "Tours Of The Homes Of The Stars". I am currently negotiating with a number of public and private bodies regarding initiating a similar venture in Dublin - Star Tour Atha Cliath.
. RTE have kindly shared their opinions on the venture, Bus Eireann have sent a man round to discuss buses with toilet facilities, and the City Manager is busy trying to interest the Dublin Tourism people.

Here's what I need from you, Mr Corah: advice on promoting the venture! You've sold both True Blue Thatcher and True Grey Major to the British punters, and over here you've helped Albert Reynolds to politically savage Dick Spring then jump into bed with him. I'm impressed.

What can you do - and what would it cost? If we can agree a figure, I believe we should go to the top people image-wise. Some preliminary headings under which we would be currently expertise-deficient include: Print or television? This summer or next? Start small with leaflets and expand? I'm sure you can add more to the list.

One initial delicate problem. My wife Dympna has studied art and, to be fair, she is quite good at drawing. However, she has composed the enclosed proposed "Logo" for the venture. Frankly, I don't like it, but I like even less the prospect of telling her so.

I'd feel on firmer ground with a few authoritative but diplomatic words from your good selves on its unsuitability. That way I can set about getting a new design without a divorce! I hope you can oblige, and I enclose £5 to cover the costs of processing this request.

Yours sincerely,

John Mackay

Mr John Mackay

PROPOSED LOGO FOR STAR TOUR ATHA CLIATH
INCORPORATING STARS, LUXURY COACH, TWO
TOURIST CAMERAS, COMBINED HOUSE & TV SET
WITH FRONT GARDEN, PLUS NAMES AND LOGOS OF
BUS EIREANN, RTE AND DUBLIN CORPORATION
(RTE LOGO USED TWICE FOR VISUAL BALANCE)

Salem Court
Maxwell Road
Dublin 6

Salem Court
Maxwell Road
Dublin 6

27 September 1993

Noel McMahon
Chief Executive
Advertising Standards Authority
IPC House
35/39 Shelbourne Road
Dublin 4

Dear Mr McMahon,

Re: Startour Atha Cliath

I wrote over three months ago to Saatchi and Saatchi Advertising in the above matter, and have still to receive a reply. Perhaps you might ask some of your people to look into the matter informally with a view to putting the wheels back on the plan before a formal complaint becomes necessary.

Yours sincerely,

John Mackay

Mr John Mackay

In reply please quote
Our Ref: ASAI/NMcM.am

IPC HOUSE,
35/39 SHELBOURNE RD.,
DUBLIN 4.
TELEPHONE (01)-608766
FAX   (01)-608113

11th October 1993

Mr John Mackay,

Salem Court,
DUBLIN 6.

Dear Mr Mackay,

We received your letter of 27th September 1993 about "Startour Atha
Cliath".

As you may know the function of the Advertising Standards Authority
for Ireland is to ensure that advertisers comply with the
requirements of the Code and to investigate complaints concerning
advertisements which are considered to be in breach of the Code.
Our responsibility is however limited to controlling the content of
advertisements.

We have no record of having received an earlier communication from
you. We made enquiries of Saatchi & Saatchi Advertising and they
have indicated that they have no information about the subject of
your letter.

I regret that it is not possible to be of greater assistance to you
in this matter.

Yours sincerely,

Noel McMahon,
CHIEF EXECUTIVE.

Chairman:
Dr. Joseph C. McGough, K.M., S.C.
Chief Executive and Secretary:
Noel McMahon
Registered in Dublin No. 82219.

                                                              Salem Court
                                                            Maxwell Road
Mr Alan McCarthy   Dublin 6
Chief Executive, Bord Trachtala
Merrion Hall, Strand Road   28 June 1993
Sandymount

Dear Mr McCarthy,

                          DOGFOOD BOWLS

   No doubt you are aware that Kiaran McGowan and Colm Mac Fhionnlaoich
at the IDA have been working for some time on an enquiry into the potential
commercial viability of manufacturing Irish-made dogfood bowls modelled
as plexiglass dinner plates.
   I am the principal in the venture, and the viability enquiry was
instigated by the Taoiseach, Mr Albert Reynolds TD, who is being kept
up to date on progress by Mr Jim Stafford in his office.
   I'm currently test-feeding various size prototype bowls with various
size dogs, and The IDA have pointed me in your direction for:

   (1) Current size of the Irish dogbowl and related market;
   (2) Sample trade and media adverts for current dogbowls and related
        products, either here or abroad.

   Another thought: certain dogs (German Shepherds, Great Danes, Irish
Wolfhounds etc) are marketed by nationality. Perhaps you could check
whether this has any equivalence in the dogbowl area? If not, we could
get in first with an imaginative nationally-identifiable product name
such as "the Irish-Wolf-It-Down-Hound-Bowl".
   I look forward to hearing from you, Mr McCarthy, and to a continuation
of the excellent assistance I have received from the IDA - it shows the
political chihuahuas who seek to muzzle your work that their ideological
bark is worse than the State's entrepreneurial bite!

   Yours sincerely,

   John Mackay

   Mr John Mackay

Merrion Hall
Strand Road
Sandymount
Dublin 4 Ireland
PO Box 203

Telephone 353 1 269 5011
Fax 353 1 269 5820

An Bord Tráchtála / The Irish Trade Board

Mr. John Mackay

Salem Court
Maxwell Road
Dublin 6.

12 July 1993

Dear Mr. Mackay,

                    Re: Dogfood Bowls

I refer to your recent letter to our Chief Executive,
Mr. Alan McCarthy. He has passed your letter to me for action.

You raised a number of marketing research issues in your letter,
many of which I feel could be adequately addressed by use of our
Market Information Centre, located in our Head Office here in
Merrion Hall. In order to facilitate our clients carrying out
research we ask, where possible, that you call in advance to make
an appointment in order to ensure that adequate facilities are
available to you.

On the broader issue of your product marketing and specifically
segmentation I feel we could best address this issue by a meeting.
I would be grateful if you could give me a call in order that we
could arrange a mutually convenient appointment.

I feel the two-prong approach of the Market Information Centre and
a meeting should help us to get to the root of many of the core
issues you have outlined in your letter.

Yours sincerely,

John Mc Cann,
Senior Marketing Specialist
East Region

Salem Court
Maxwell Road
Dublin 6

1 September 1993

Mr Peter Cassells
General Secretary
Irish Congress of Trade Unions
Liberty Hall
Dublin 1

Dear Mr Cassells,

Can I first express my outrage at the recent venomous attacks by the multi-jobbing Fine Gael Senator Shane Ross on your well-deserved and hard-earned exorbitant salaries as union officials.

Where would we, the Irish workers, be without your class leadership? Ask the now destitute English miners who so gutlessly turned their ideological backs on Arthur Scargill, only to find Thatcher's dagger firmly lodged between their ribs and their paypacket.

You are our leaders, and we have none better, and you must be paid much more than us if you are to be able to fight effectively for our pay to stay the same. I enclose a token £5 donation towards the struggle for job protection - I'm sure the Pat The Striker fund could do with some extra dough!

I am also writing because some colleagues and I are trying to raise funds for a statue to commemorate the recent Irish Everest expedition. As next year is the 25th anniversary of the first man on the moon, we hope that the statue will jointly commemorate both events.

Our fundraising plan is for Dawson Stelfox to climb Liberty Hall while dressed as Spiderman, and be greeted at the top by the American Ambassador attired as Wonderwoman. We hope that you will let us use Liberty Hall, and we would be delighted if you would personally complete the symbolic roof-top trio dressed perhaps as an Irish Leprechaun or whatever else you may feel more appropriate.

We will await the necessary permission before advancing the project further.

Yours sincerely,

John Mackay

John Mackay

Irish Congress of Trade Unions

19 Raglan Road, Dublin 4

Our Reference: 7010

9 September 1993

Mr John Mackay

Salem Court
Maxwell Road
DUBLIN 6

Dear John

Many thanks for your smart-aleky letter, but I am afraid you were too smart. Shane Ross's article was about <u>SIPTU</u> in <u>Liberty Hall</u>, not Congress at 19 Raglan Road.

Since my salary comes nowhere near the figures quoted by Senator Ross, Shane Ross's salary and indeed maybe your own, I was tempted to hold on to the £5, but I am sure you know more worthy causes.

Yours sincerely

Peter Cassells

Peter Cassells
General Secretary
PC/ag

Noel Pearson
Ferndale Films
4 Harcourt Terrace
Dublin 2

Salem Court
Maxwell Road
Dublin 6

10 August 1993

Dear Mr Pearson,

Here is a draft outline for a screenplay - it is a minimalist treatment, but I am sure you will see its potential and I enclose a stamped addressed envelope for any constructive criticisms you may have.

MY BACK GARDEN

A child, born wheelchair-bound, overcomes prejudice and adversity through personal courage and the unbending support of his extended family.

An English cousin, a secret transvestite, inherits the family's Dublin house and threatens to renovate and sell it - but our hero resists and plans the perfect murder.

After visiting a faith healer, he haltingly walks from his wheelchair, triumphantly smiles, and stampedes a herd of horses to push his cockney cousin over a cliff at the bottom of the back garden.

When the police arrive, he is sitting innocently, immobile in his wheelchair; as the credits roll, the camera zooms in on his pocket, from which a plane ticket to Lourdes is protruding.

What do you think, Mr Pearson? I have never written a screenplay before, and I would greatly appreciate your advice and guidance. I enclose £5 to cover any postage or administrative costs, and I look forward to hearing your criticism.

Yours sincerely,

John Mackay

Mr John Mackay

Salem Court
Maxwell Road
Dublin 6

24 September 1993

Mr Jerry Kelly
Ulster Television
Havelock House
Ormeau Road
Belfast

Dear Jerry,

I've always admired your readiness to make an eejit of yourself on TV, dropping your bags on camera, playing the "oafish" Ulsterman, and making faces behind the backs of intellectuals.

Jerry, do you want a real laugh on your show? My wife Dympna's mum Maisie, who was born in Tyrone, now lives in a home for the elderly bewildered outside Dublin where she keeps both the inmates and the keepers in stitches with a stand-up routine playing the tin whistle and telling jokes.

Most of the gags are gentle, colloquial ribbing, apart from one frankly disgusting joke which she heard from a Sailor in a Belfast pub – I think DuBarrys – in the 1950's. She then plays a clever medley of "The Sash" followed by "Kevin Barry" and closes her tin whistle symphony with the Chinese national anthem "The East is Red".

Her incontinence is only a problem at night and, kept away from drink, she is the sort of "character" who would shine on your show. I'll check with our insurance man, but she should be covered by her own policy if anything unfortunate were to happen on air.

Would she need to do a "screen test"? We're often in Belfast. Drop us a line and we'll call in at your convenience.

Yours sincerely,

John Mackay

Mr John Mackay

PS While I have your ear, is there any chance of a signed photo of your good self on the studio couch? I enclose £5 to cover any administrative costs.

Salem Court
Maxwell Road
Dublin 6

Joan Burton
Minister of State
Department of Social Welfare
Leinster House
Dublin 1

27 September 1993

Dear Ms Burton,

Congratulations on your performance on Questions And Answers and, in particular, your eloquent defence of the voluntary student workfare scheme which my daughter Susie availed of this Summer.

Susie was delighted with the job opportunity which the scheme gave her - the type of job which, as you so rightly said, is so often given to family members. She was a Dail secretary! No, I'm only joking, of course. The Dail doesn't sit during the Summer!

Seriously, though, you're doing an excellent job in defending policies that must be hard to defend, but you're on a winner with the voluntary student workfare scheme. I've voted for Labour all of my life and I enclose a token donation to your next election campaign fund.

While I have your attention, Joan, could you settle a small family debate which centres around your good self? My wife Dympna heard from a neighbour who is a Labour Party member that you decided to enter politics while playing a game of Trivial Pursuits in Nairobi. Is this true?

There's a fiver on the outcome!

Yours sincerely,

John Mackay

Mr John Mackay

Mr. John Mackay,

Salem Court,
Maxwell Road,   6 October, 1993.
Dublin 6.

Dear John,

Thank you for your letter of 27 September 1993 and for your very welcome donation to the Labour Party funds in Dublin West which I have passed on to the Constituency Treasurer.

The Student's Scheme for the summer was, I think, a very interesting experiment and I think it gives us some lessons for the future. I hope that the scheme can be expanded and improved and we are currently carrying out an evaluation of how the scheme worked, both from the point of students and from the point of view of the Sponsoring Organisations; so if your daughter has any detailed comments to make on the scheme, I would be interested to hear them.

In relation to your last point, I certainly didn't decide to enter politics as a consequence of playing Trivial Pursuits in Nairobi. I have been involved in the Labour Party as an active worker for the Party on policy issues since finishing my education. What I said in the book "The Women who Won", Una Claffey's book, was that I made a decision about running for electoral office partly as a response to a truth game which was run in Nairobi by an American with whom I was friendly at the time. I certainly consider myself to be a political activist for a very long period of time, but I didn't necessarily see myself as an electoral politician.

Anyway, that's what the story is. Thank you again for your good wishes.

Yours sincerely

JOAN BURTON T.D.
Minister of State

Salem Court
Maxwell Road
Dublin 6

9 March 1993

Liam Brady
Manager
Glasgow Celtic FC
Glasgow
Scotland

Dear Liam,

I hope you don't mind me calling you Liam, but like so many who have followed your fortunes at Arsenal, Italy, West Ham and Glasgow, I feel I know you more intimately than a "Dear Mr Brady" would reflect. Quite simply, never has the green shirt of Ireland been donned by a classier player.

So your on-field excellence has yet to manifest itself in the Celtic manager's office. Never mind; few in world football have emulated the ease with which Franz Beckenbaur and Turlough O'Connor made the shift from playing to managerial success.

So keep the chin up, Chippy - football is football; if it weren't, it wouldn't be football. Just try to recapture the ambition and passion you showed during your many lire-making moves from club to club, and get your players to give the same total loyalty to the green and white hoops of Celtic. Go for it!

Anyway, Liam, I was hoping you could settle an ongoing argument between myself and a "drinking buddy" in Dublin. A cousin of mine went to St Aidans CBS in Whitehall, Dublin, and says you were expelled for refusing to play for the school's gaelic football team.

I have heard, however, from a usually reliable source in the Dublin media, that you were actually expelled for deliberately "mis-hitting" a shot to render painful a delicate anatomical part of one of the school's Christian Brothers.

Which of us is right? There's a fiver on the outcome!

Yours faithfully,

John Mackay

Mr John Mackay

The Celtic Football and Athletic Company Limited

95 Kerrydale Street Glasgow G40 3RE
Telex: 931 2100437 BW
Fax: 041-551 8106
Telephone: 041-556 2611

Our Ref: LB/CD

16 March 1993

J Mackay Esq

Salem Court
Maxwell Road
DUBLIN 6

Dear John

I acknowledge receipt of your letter of 9 March 1993. With regard to your argument, all I can say is that your cousin's version is the correct one.

Thank you for your best wishes and good luck.

Kind regards

Yours sincerely

LIAM BRADY
FOOTBALL MANAGER

Liam Brady, MANAGER

DIRECTORS
Kevin Kelly
David D. Smith, BSc., C.A.
John C. McGinn
James M. Farrell, M.A., LL.B.
Christopher D. White, B.A., C.A.
Thomas J. Grant
Michael Kelly, C.B.E., O.St.J., J.P., B.Sc.(Econ)., Ph.D., LL.D., D.L., F.C.I.M.

UMBRO
OFFICIAL KIT SPONSORS

Registered Office, Celtic Park, Glasgow-G40 3RE.
Registered No. 3487 Scotland. VAT Reg. No. 260 2974 61.

John Bowman
Questions and Answers
RTE
Donnybrook
Dublin 4

Dear Mr Bowman,

Firstly, your programme is excellent – a worthy advertisement for the national channel and a "must-see" amongst a sea of mediocrity.

However, I have been in correspondence (copy attached) with newly elected Green Party TD Trevor Sargent, who points out that you only gave him ONE HOUR's notice to appear on your programme some weeks ago. I might remind you that he was also placed in the audience rather than the panel.

What is happening here? he's new and young, but deserves respect. I pay my TV licence, I voted Green Party last time out, and I don't think I'm being unfair when I say that I think an an explanation is warranted.

Again, congratulations on an otherwise excellent and always incisive programme.

Yours sincerely,

John Mackay

Mr John Mackay

PS I enclose a stamped addressed envelope as I know you must be busy.

Salem Court
Maxwell Road
Dublin 6

18 May 1993

John Bowman
Questions and Answers
RTE, Donnybrook
Dublin 4

Dear Mr Bowman,

I assume you are a wealthy man; you are never off TV, you wear expensive ties, and you write for "serious" newspapers across the water. Perhaps 32p means little to you, but to Green voters it represents nearly a third of a pound.

Mr Bowman, I wrote to you over TEN WEEKS ago to ask why you placed Trevor Sargent TD in the audience of your show rather than the panel. I have heard NOTHING to date, and I hope that the stamp I enclosed has not been "pocketed".

Yours sincerely,

John Mackay

Mr Mackay

Dublin 4, Ireland
Telephone 01 643111
Telefax 01 643080
Telex 93700
Direct Line 01 64

Baile Átha Cliath 4, Éire
Telefón 01 643111
Telefax 01 643080
Teleics 93700
Líne Díreach 01 64

Radio Telefís Éireann

June 22nd 1993

Dear Mr Mackay,

Thank you for your enquiry re Trevor Sargent and Questions and Answers and apologies for any delay in my response. I too was surprised to find Trevor Sargent in the audience of the programme. I think the Greens as a party may have been invited to accept two audience tickets and they selected him.

I agree with you that it would be more appropriate for him to be on the panel rather than in the audience and have no doubt that that is where he will be when he next appears on the programme.

We have many requests for panel seats from independents and smaller parties and, although we have often received complaints from them that they are squeezed out by the larger parties, our figures show that they are well represented on our panels.

Thanking you for your kind comments on the programme.

Yours sincerely,

John Bowman

Salem Court
Maxwell Road
Dublin 6

18 May 1993

The Ambassador to Ireland
The British Embassy
33 Merrion Road
Dublin 4

Dear Ambassador,

In the great see-saw of Anglo-Irish relations over the past 800 years, I was most impressed by your willingness to jail the tax evading jockey Lester Piggot. Outrageously, this man would have walked free in Ireland, and would probably by now have bought shares in Greencore or a "bargain" apartment in Mespil Road.

You've been here a while, and you know what Ireland is like. The great and the golden bask in the self-perpetuating lifestyle of insider share and property deals; the rest of us toil for a pittance or take our place at the back of the dole queue. Ambassador, I've had enough.

I am writing to enquire about the possibility of claiming economic refugee status in your country. I understand that, under EC law, I can receive dole payments in Britain. Is this true? If so, how much would I get and what are the conditions?

Also, do you provide Assisted Passage or Resettlement Grants for economic refugees? I know that the EC is giving Ireland IR£8 billion. My share of Britain's contribution to this would be about IR£200. I could even pay this back by delaying my move for a while, thus saving you the dole money you would have been paying me.

Ambassador, I am prepared to work hard and be a good British citizen. Please give me the chance.

Yours sincerely,

John Mackay

Mr John Mackay

PS Can you send me any money "up-front" for further research?

21 May 1993

British Embassy
Dublin

31/33 Merrion Road
Dublin 4

Mr J Mackay

Telephone: 2695211
Telex: 93717 (a/b 93717 UKDB EI)
Facsimile: 2 838 423 Group 3

Salem Court
Maxwell Road
DUBLIN 6

Dear Mr Mackay

Thank you for your letter of 18 May.

The UN definition of a refugee, accepted by the UK, is a person who suffers a well founded fear of persecution in his or her own country. People who believe that they would benefit economically by living in another country are not classified as refugees. Since we do not accept the status of economic refugee, it follows that we also do not provide assisted passage or resettlement grants to them.

However, EC citizens are eligible to live and work in the United Kingdom. EC citizens living in the UK who meet the conditions are eligible for the same social security provisions as UK citizens. Your local social welfare office should be able to provide details of eligibility.

However, I would strongly recommend that, before travelling to the UK, you ensure that you have a job to go to. The Irish Department of Enterprise and Employment can advise you on work opportunities in the UK. I regret that we have no funds to assist you with further research.

Yours sincerely,

Alan Cobden

Salem Court
Maxwell Road
Dublin 6

11 June 1993

Peter Barry TD
Leinster House
Dublin 2

Dear Mr Barry,

Or should I call you Reynard, the silver fox? For years, I followed the playful antics of the chimps on the TV advert for Barrys tea. I was puzzled by the anthropoid representations, until it struck me like a thunderbolt; the subliminal symbolism was an inverted three wise men - Bruton, Dukes and Garret. In true Fine Gael fashion, I had missed the the blindingly obvious - grey hair equals grey matter, dusted with experience and topped off with common sense.

You have been to the fore where it matters: transport and power, education, environment, and Anglo-Irish contretemps. I urge you, Peter, it's not too late. Throw your trilby in the ring, save Fine Gael and Ireland from bungling fools, and allow the one party which understands business and probity to get its hands where they belong - on the tiller of the ship of state. You have the presence to make our pathetic political pirates walk the plank; I enclose a token donation to help launch your bid for glory, our hope for salvation.

Incidentally, can I borrow a small cup of sugar from that silo of solid reliability? I refer to a matter concerning which my good wife Dympna occasionally chides me. I have never been able to get comfortably fitting dentures, and often watch the box with the molars grinning from a glass beside me. Just after the weather, which follows the nine o'clock RTE news, Dympna always brings me in a cup of your best Barry's Gold along with a couple of custard creams.

My query, Peter: is it considered acceptable manners to dunk the biscuits in the tea while in the company of others? An early reply from a man in your position tea-wise may be the sugarcube that re-sweetens our familial relationship.

Yours sincerely,

John Mackay

Mr John Mackay

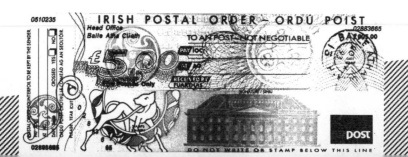

DÁIL ÉIREANN
BAILE ÁTHA CLIATH, 2.
(Dublin, 2).

Peter Barry T.D.
Blackrock
Cork

20 August 1993

Mr. John Mackay,

Salem Court,
Maxwell Road,
Dublin 6.

_____

Dear Mr. Mackay,

My very sincere apologies for not replying to your letter of June 11. It is only when I received your letter of August 10 that I realised there was a subscription of £5.00 enclosed for which I thank you.

I frankly didn't reply to your earlier letter as I wasn't sure whether you were 'pulling my leg' regarding dunking your biscuits in tea (and here my answer is - do whatever pleases you) and assuming the leadership of Fine Gael.

I offered myself for the leadership of Fine Gael in 1987 when Garret Fitzgerald resigned and even at that stage I thought, because of the intense pressures on politicians at the top level, that I might be too old. Six years on I am certainly too old but I appreciate and am flattered by your suggestion.

Despite my very poor record in responding to your letter please continue to write with any suggestions you may have on either tea or politics.

Yours sincerely,

PETER BARRY T.D.

Salem Court
Maxwell Road
Dublin 6

18 October 1993

Noel Smyth
Noel Smyth and Partners
Solicitors
22 Fitzwilliam Square
Dublin 2

Dear Mr Smyth,

When I read about your selfless service to the Dunnes, I concluded that
Noel Smyth's family values matched John Mackay's - an unemployed
"working" man, currently between entrepreneurial challenges.

Rather than sit on my hands and mope like some no-hoper, I have decided
to "go for it" and organise the last asset over which I have any effective
control: my family.

As a family man, a business high flyer and a wizard tax expert, Noel,
could you advise me on the ups and downs of incorporating our "nuclear"
family into a limited liability company? I see myself as Chief Executive
and Chairman, my wife Dympna as Company Secretary, my son Tobias, 22, and
daughter Susie, 17, non-executive directors.

Mr Smyth, would it be more tax efficient for an unemployed father-of-
two to be a company director rather than an ordinary Joe, maybe having
my dole payments classified as "expenses" or whatever?

You have given many of us "little guys" with more faith than prospects
some hope for this country. I enclose £5 as a down payment for your advice.

God Bless You, Mr Smyth,

Yours sincerely,

John Mackay

Mr John Mackay

Mr John Hume MP, MEP
Leader SDLP
Derry
Northern Ireland

Salem Court
Maxwell Road
Dublin 6

24 September 1993

Dear Mr Hume,

You are the greatest Irish politician of our generation, so don't let the political pygmies poison your intellectual water-hole: as Churchill said, "Blah, Blah is betta than Wa, Wa".

However, I must say that, although you recently lost weight and have a nice new navy suit, your hair still sometimes looks like an unmade bed when you appear on the telly.

As an international statesman, you will know that President Clinton's fortunes turned around when he had his hair cut by Cristophe, the Belgian crimper. Likewise Mr Desmond O' Malley, whose own unruly thatch was not unlike your own, saw his career progress down the democratic fast-lane after he had a cut, wash and set.

I enclose £5 towards the cost of a good clip and style: there are no prizes for coming second on the pan-fashionalist front!

Yours sincerely,

John Mackay

Mr John Mackay

Salem Court
Maxwell Road
Dublin 6

The Secretary   11 June 1993
Fitzwilliam Lawn Tennis Club
Dublin 4

Dear Sir,

Knowing of Fitzwilliam's reputation, I'm sure you will appreciate my
opening this letter with a little joke attributed to the former British
government minister, Alan Clarke. When faced with a male Departmental
Secretary on his appointment, Mr Clarke (the son of Lord Clarke of
Civilisation) quipped, "Do you take dictation?"

Anyway, I recently returned to this country after accumulating some
capital abroad. After sorting out my business affairs, I am now settling
my social arrangements, and, following some reassuring publicity, I
believe your "men only" club would meet my requirements.

I expect "the lads" have some "rare oul times" at Fitzwilliam, sipping
sundowners in a bar uncluttered with flibberty-gibbet lasses chattering
on about this and that. I like men's talk: politics, business, sport,
telling an occasional risque joke without having to look over one's
shoulder to check if some femme fatale is within earshot.

However, don't let there be any misunderstanding: John Mackay is a red-
blooded, rarin' to rave, heterosexual male. If the "lads" at Fitwilliam
wish to have an "exotic dancer" in to entertain at a stag dinner, I will
be first on my feet if they ask for a "volunteer" to be the vamp's victim.
No, John MacKay is not a spoil-sport, but a man. Say no more.

If there is some sort of membership vetting procedure, I would
appreciate it if you could "handle" it for me. If the committee needs
persuading, I enclose £5 for you to buy drinks for reluctant members.
If you need more money, for this or that, let me know and I'll oblige
in an instant.

Yours sincerely,

John Mackay

Mr John Mackay

Fitzwilliam Lawn Tennis Club,
Appian Way,
Dublin 6.
Telephone 603988
Fax 617156

23rd June, 1993.

Mr. John Mackay,

Salem Court,
Maxwell Road,
<u>DUBLIN 6</u>.

Dear Mr. Mackay,

Thank you for your letter of the 11th June. I regret to inform you that membership is closed at present and as we do not keep a waiting list I am returning your £5 postal order which is enclosed.

Yours sincerely,

GARY HOLOHAN,
Hon. Secretary.

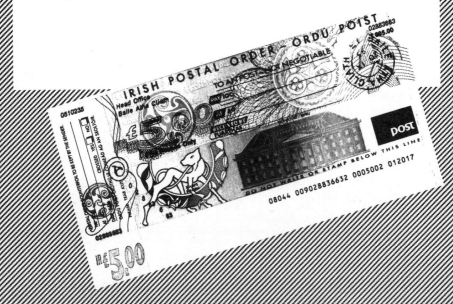

Salem Court
Maxwell Road
Dublin 6

Prionsias de Rossa TD
Leader, Democratic Left
Leinster House
Dublin 2

17 Feb 1993

Dear Mr de Rossa,

A belated well done! I refer to your courageous decision to leave the European Parliament to campaign against European unity. Your principled stand was internationally vindicated by the resounding Danish "nein" to German economic domination, and domestically proven by the recent currency chaos supported by all of the right wing parties.

Yet, when we had a chance last year to vote on whether we should hand over our hard-earned sovereignty to the Bundesbank, only the Democratic Left and the pro-lifers were prepared to defend Irish nationalism.

Congratulations also on leaving in your wake the dubious counterfeit communists who once were your colleagues. You may or may not in your day have knowingly or unknowingly signed or not signed requests for money you knew nothing about, but frankly I don't care - you are clearly now aware that social democracy, not socialist drivel, is the future. Yet - yet, yet, yet, indeed - how many of your current colleagues are still under the spell of Marxist ideology?

As you and Dick both know, we need to redistribute the votes before we can redistribute the wealth - though, in the area of wealth redistribution, your dogged former deputy in Dublin North East, legal eagle Pat MacCartan (who lives near my cousin in Terenure) is an example to us all of upwardly mobile egalitarianism! Well done, Pat.

Anyway, here's the point. I, like you, am a modern social democrat, aware of the dangers of European unity, though up to now politically uninvolved. I have recently returned to Ireland after a turn abroad, and am looking for a principled political home. What exactly do you offer? Please send me details. I enclose a token donation to the Party by way of indicating my commitment. Also, should I join, what arrangements should I make to contribute regularly to the party by standing order? I look forward to hearing from you.

Yours sincerely,

John Mackay

Mr John Mackay

DÁIL ÉIREANN

BAILE ÁTHA CLIATH, 2.
(Dublin, 2).

26 February 1993

Mr. J. McKay

Salem Court
Maxwell Road
Dublin 6

Dear Mr. McKay

Thank you for your letter and donation of £5, which is very much appreciated.

I enclose a document on our Party's constitution, rules and politics, which will, I am sure help to clarify the positions of Democratic Left. If there are other queries concerning our policies, let me know.

The membership fee for persons who are working is £5 per year. Members and supporters who can afford it are asked to make a contribution by Standing Order for any amount that suits their pocket. We can discuss that again if you decide that we are the party you wish to support.

Yours sincerely

PR de Rossa

PROINSIAS DE ROSSA T.D.
LEADER
DEMOCRATIC LEFT

DEMOCRATIC **left**

10/3/93

Thanking you for Donation,

marie Brady

Head Office:
69 Middle Abbey Street
Dublin 1 ◆ Ireland
Tel: (01) 729550
Fax: (01) 729238

Dáil Office:
Leinster House
Dublin 2 ◆ Ireland
Tel: (01) 789911
Fax: (01) 789119

WITH COMPLIMENTS

Salem Court
Maxwell Road
Dublin 6

14 October 1993

The Chairman
Womens Political Associaton
c/o the Council for
the Status of Women
64 Lower Mount Street
Dublin 2

Dear Chairman,

On RTE radio recently, Frances FitzGerald reminded us of the role women played in resolving the Palestine-Israeli problem - I understand she indicated that they had made the tea and sandwiches - and then last week the Irish Hospice held a nationwide coffee morning to raise funds. Mixing both ideas, I thought of a plan - "CAN DO!" (Coffee mornings Against the National Debt Organisation). If there are, say, a million housewives in the country, and each one held a coffee morning every week for two years, we could raise up to a billion pounds!

We could get Bewleys to sponsor the coffee, go to Gateaux for cakes and Jacobs for biscuits. And start it all off by hiring the Point Depot in Dublin for The Mother of All Coffee Mornings. If we were to get a few "partners", as I understand husbands are now called, to do the washing up, my "partner" John has a contact in Fairy Liquid who he could speak to for materials.

Would the WPA be able to act as a matron for such an initiative? I look forward to hearing from you.

Yours sincerely,

Dympna Mackay

Mrs Dympna Mackay

Salem Court
Maxwell Road
Dublin 6

Mons Jacques Delors
President
EC Commission
Brussels

26 July 1993

Dear Mr Delors,

Bonjour! Comment allez-vouz? Vive la France! Ooh la la! And merci beaucoup for leaving your sick-bed to smite the Scottish accountant Millen. You brilliantly blocked his miserly attempts to claw back Ireland's £8 billion bonanza to a fairer allocation.

And your pragmatic massaging of the números made our begging-bowl balance look a bouncing billion punts more than it is!

Jacques, I wrote some time ago requesting IR£2,000 as my portion of Ireland's £8 billion. Your Mr Boyd politely replied that the cash must go to useful projects, approved by the Commission, and that my personal bank account was unlikely to qualify for same.

Though disappointed, I asked myself: how would Jacques Delors react to such a petite difficulté? Would he throw in his Euro-towel and lie prostrate on his sick-bed? Non, I replied, Jacques Delors would bounce back fighting and adapt to the nouveau realité.

And so I have devised a useful project for your consideration. It is an Irish Euro-Calendar, with each month illustrated by a picture highlighting the unique relationship between Ireland and one of the twelve EC member states. I enclose details of the proposed pictures, which would be photographed on location, using professional models dressed where relevant in appropriate national attire.

Please send details on combien cash vouz can donnez-moi, and where je can get it. Again, merci beaucoup; I look forward to hearing from you, and I enclose £5 to help with postage and administration costs.

Yours sincerely,

John Mackay

Mr John Mackay

PS Regards to Mr Boyd and everyone else dans le bureau.

PROPOSED THEMES FOR
PICTORIAL REPRESENTATION
ON PROPOSED IRISH
EURO-CALENDAR FOR 1994

Salem Court
Maxwell Road
Dublin 6

**JANUARY
(IRELAND)**

An emerald-clad
leprechaun happily
dancing among a
field of shamrock
with a bishop and a
comely maiden

**FEBRUARY
(BRITAIN)**

English football
fans behaving
sportingly as their
team loses yet
another World Cup
qualifying game

**MARCH
(PORTUGAL)**

Shiploads of sea-
faring explorers
setting sail to
discover new lands
for the Irish to
emigrate to

**APRIL
(FRANCE)**

Paris in the Spring
and Dick Spring in
Paris canvassing
support for more
Euro-money for
Ireland

**MAY
(ITALY)**

Olé Olé Olé Olé!
Jack's army in the
paradise land of
the papacy, soccer,
great drink and no
government

**JUNE
(SPAIN)**

Hundreds of happy
Spanish students
chattering noisily
as they clutter up
our streets and
public transport

SUBMITTED TO MONS JAQUES DELORS,
EC PRESIDENT, AS A USEFUL PROJECT
FOR CONSIDERATION FOR A SHARE OF
IRELAND'S £8 BILLION EURO-BONANZA

**JULY
(HOLLAND)**

King William of
Orange leaving his
windmill to lay
Dutch claim to a
third of the Irish
tricolour

**AUGUST
(GERMANY)**

Rows of industrious
early-rising German
tourists relaxing
in their deckchairs
along Dollymount
strand

**SEPTEMBER
(GREECE)**

Mary Robinson as
Shirley Valentine
choosing poverty
and sun in Greece
instead of poverty
and rain in Ireland

**OCTOBER
(LUXEMBOURG)**

The inside of the
studio of Radio
Luxembourg, with
Ireland's latest
winning Eurovision
song playing

**NOVEMBER
(DENMARK)**

Hans Christian
Anderson telling a
fairy tale about
Denmark halting the
Maastricht Treaty
with a referendum

**DECEMBER
(BELGIUM)**

Christmas time!
We wait for Santa
to arrive from
Brussels with loads
of Euro-cash and
other presents

Salem Court
Maxwell Road
Dublin 6

27 September 1993

Mons Jacques Delors
President
EC Commission
Brussels

Dear Mr Delors,

I wrote two months ago (copy enclosed) with a proposal (un proposal)
for a Euro-calendar to be financed by the Maastricht millions.
Quelle surprise! I have received no reply. Perhaps the £5 I enclosed
to cover postage and administrative costs was insufficient.
If so, here's un autre fiver.
I look forward to hearing from you.
Merci beaucoup.

Yours sincerely,

John Mackay

Mr John Mackay

COMMISSION OF THE EUROPEAN COMMUNITIES

Office of the President

Brussels, 0 7 -10- 1993
SG(93)D/86434/87882

Dear Mr Mackay,

President Delors has asked me to thank you for your letter of 26 July 1993, in which you ask for financial support in exchange for a Euro-Calendar you sent him, and your reminder letter of 27 September.

Your letter was much funnier than what he usually receives and I congratulate you on your knowledge of Molière's language. I enjoyed your calendar, but I am sorry I have to confirm that you cannot expect any personal financial assistance from the Commission. EC Structural Funds are not designed to help individual citizens, but to finance projects which address the recipient countries' development problems - such as road building, the purchase of telecommunications equipment, projects to improve the quality of the environment, the promotion of industrial activities in less developed regions, etc. All supported operations must be in accordance with pre-established conditions enshrined in EC legislation and agreements between the Community and the Member States. All projects must be supported by the relevant Member State.

As you may have guessed, your work, which is of a less practical nature, does not qualify for support under these tight rules.

I am nevertheless certain that you will appreciate the benefits which EC support will indirectly bring to you, as indeed to all Irish citizens.

I am sending back your two £ 5 mail orders. It was a pleasure reading your letter, so I did it for free ! I am also enclosing the stamps you sent: in any case, they cannot be used in Belgium.

Yours sincerely,

Christopher BOYD

Mr John MACKAY

Salem Court
Maxwell Road
IRL - DUBLIN 6

Rue de la Loi 200 - B-1049 Brussels, Belgium - Office:
Telephone: direct line (+32-2)29...... exchange 299.11.11 -
Telex: COMEU B 21877 - Telegraphic address: COMEUR Brussels

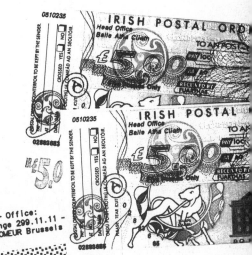

Salem Court
Maxwell Road
Dublin 6
Republic of Ireland

11 July 1993

Baroness Thatcher
House of Lords
Westminster Palace
Westminster
London SW1

Dear Lady Thatcher,

The entrepreneurial spirit (a vying breed!) fostered by you through the Thatcher Age was adopted by this family on the smaller island in the social suburbia of north-western Europe. And it is with your economic miracle in mind that we now ask you to trade with us!

Back in 1981 when the little Haughey fellow was Emperor here (I believe you called him a barrow boy, very droll) he visited you at Number 10 and presented you with a silver Georgian tea pot. Anyway, some weeks ago my lady wife, Dympna, was rooting around a distress sale of some minor aristocrisy here (Lloyds names, I understand) and she came across a silver Georgian cream jug and sugar bowl — companion pieces to the tea pot given to you by little Haughey.

Naturally, we didn't tell the silly old trout in charge of their significance and picked them up at the right price (buy low, sell high – the Thatcher way). And, in its own way, this now-complete tea set is a symbol of Thatcherism, a microcosm of an idealised international free market: both of us has a commodity the other desires — our only quibble is the price!

So, we hope you will agree to sell us the tea pot (it must bring back terrible memories for you every time you look at it). On the other hand, you may have some sentimental attachment to the tea pot and wish to purchase the cream jug and sugar bowl. If so, we're open to offers. Can we do business? I enclose £5 as a luck-of-the-Irish pump primer.

Yours sincerely,

John MacKay

Mr John MacKay

PS Please keep hammering away (Out! Out! Out!) at the sick socialistic Maastricht dictat; if it fails, our left-led governing lackeys may have to trade in their Euro-begging bowl for a work ethic!

PPS Love to Dennis and the twins.

Salem Court
Maxwell Road
Dublin 6

27 September 1993

Mr Mark Worthington
The Thatcher Foundation
PO Box 1466
London SW1 X9HY
England

Dear Mr Worthington,

Further to our telephone conversation today, perhaps you could take over the reins on the matter of the unanswered letter I wrote to Lady Thatcher last July?

I enclose another £5 towards the Thatcher Foundation, an institution that, like its founder, can transform humankind as we know it and lay a basis for a New World Order based on Commerce Sans Frontieres!

Yours sincerely,

John Mackay

Mr John Mackay

29th September,1993

Dear Mr.MacKay,

Thank you for your letter to Lady Thatcher regarding
the gift she received from Mr.Haughey.   I regret the
delay in replying.

I have now had the opportunity to discuss this matter
with Lady Thatcher and she remembers the gift well.
However, gifts given to a Prime Minister in office do
not become their possessions and, when we left Downing
Street, Mr.Haughey's gift was left there as part of the
official fabric of the house.

Should you wish to make any further enquiries about this
Teapot please write to No.10 Downing Street.   I am
returning your Postal Order herewith and thank you for
your kind letter.

Yours sincerely,

(Mrs. C.M.Crawford, MBE)
 Personal Assistant to Lady Thatcher

John MacKay, Esq.

                                                    Salem Court
                                                    Maxwell Road
                                                    Dublin 6

Mr John Major MP   5 October 1993
Prime Minister
10 Downing Street
London SW1

Dear John,

   Many thanks for your recent letter acknowledging the financial
contribution I made to the Conservative Party. Lady Thatcher has since
suggested that I write to you regarding a business proposal which, sadly,
she had to decline.
   If you check around the house, you should find a silver Georgian tea
pot which she left behind when you moved in (she got it from our former
emperor Mr Haughey in the early 80's).
   John, I have since come into possession of the silver cream jug and
sugar bowl which make up the set. Would you like to take them off my hands,
or would you rather I make an offer on the tea pot, which must be of little
(or indeed, negative) sentimental value to your good self?
   As you no doubt know, I am of means, and a quick deal with me tea pot
wise could considerably fatten the Treasury's chest.
   Give me a shout after you check what's best with young Portillo.

   Yours sincerely,

   John Mackay

   Mr John Mackay

Salem Court
Maxwell Road
Dublin 6

3 June 1993

The Manager
Jurys Hotel
Ballsbridge
Dublin 4

Dear Mr Ducie,

I understand that the lawyers and judges, who were an integral part of an evening's entertainment at the Shelbourne, no longer patronise the premises following recent unfortunate publicity.

This, I believe, leaves a hole in the market which Jurys could breach: it would not compete with, but complement, Hal Roach or whoever you have on in the cabaret, bringing in an extra "set" of punters.

I have a cousin, Freddie, who was always an excellent mimic and very demonstrative at school, and he and I have come up with a "knockabout" routine which we could perform in the lounge, lobby, or wherever it was required. We would pretend to be lawyers, laugh very loudly and use upper-crust accents on multi-syllabic words. Then, at closing time, Freddie would "grey up" and pose as an inebriate judge, demanding a drink.

It always got a laugh at the Shelbourne, and very soon the rich and famous would be calling each other on their "mobile" phones and flocking to your excellent emporium. Result? extra profit for you; artistic achievement, a weekly stipend and some free drink for us.

Mr Ducie, I look forward to hearing from you, and to commencing a mutually profitable business relationship.

Yours sincerely,

John Mackay

Mr John Mackay

PS We can audition if you wish or, better still, we could arrive unannounced and put on an "impromptu" show. Break a leg!

JURYS
HOTEL AND
TOWERS

Ballsbridge, Dublin 4, Ireland.
Telephone (01) 605000, Fax (01) 605540, Telex 93723.

Mr. John Mackay,

Salem Court,
Maxwell Road,
Dublin 6.

19th August, 1993

Dear Mr. Mackay,

Thank you for your recent letter proposing a theatrical "floor show"
in our Dubliner Bar.

I regret to advise you that I am unable to facilitate you at
present, but should the occasion arise that we are in the market
for such a show I will contact you.

Thank you for your interest.

Yours sincerely,

Joan Bennett
p/r
Seamus McGowan
Deputy General/Operations Manager

JURYS HOTEL GROUP PLC. IRELAND: DUBLIN · CORK · LIMERICK · WATERFORD. SCOTLAND: GLASGOW

⊕ Supranational
Worldwide Reservations

Salem Court
Maxwell Road
Dublin 6

18 May 1993

Mr David Kingston
Managing Director,
Irish Life Assurance PLC
Irish Life Centre
Abbey Street
Dublin 1

Dear Mr Kingston,

The dust from the razing of the Berlin Wall had barely settled when the killer virus they call the Irish left began attacking your Mespil commune system. This weak shandy, one part Franco McDowell, two parts Ho Chi Quinn, a coalition spawned in hell, would bring our greatest money spinning institution to its knees just to accomodate a few whining tenants who think that they own, not rent, their apartments.

I have it on good authority that at least one resident of the Mespil complex ran with the Spanish "republican" cause in the 1930s and for a brief period in the 1960s supported Harold Wilson's Maoist Labour Government in Britain! Now it would seem that the elevation of clever Dick Spring to Tanaiste has emboldened this individual to try to bring down Irish society as we know it – starting with an ideological levelling of the Mespil Road flats.

Sir, you have a duty to the law of the land. You did not breach the law of the land. I am of similar values, and am therefore, like your good self, of means. Please count me in should any future property deals arise with similar potential and requirements. Sir, sitting tenants do not worry me: they are nothing that a Sony stereo and a Deep Purple CD cannot sort out – remember Noriego in Panama?

It is of course important to have prior knowledge of these "super" deals. I enclose a fiver to cover the administrative costs of adding my name to your mailing list. If things work out, I'm not a greedy man; I look after the hand that feeds.

Yours sincerely,

John Mackay

Mr John Mackay

⫶ Irish Life

Irish Life Assurance plc
Irish Life Centre, Lower Abbey Street
Dublin 1, Ireland

Telephone 01 704.2000
Telex 32562 / Fax 704.1900

15th September 1993

Mr. John Mackay,

Salem Court,
Maxwell Road,
Dublin 6.

Dear Mr. Mackay,

I refer to your letters of 10th August and 18th May. Your letters indicate a view that the price at which we sold Mespil Estate in December 1992 did not reflect its true value. This is not the case as the independent valuers Lisney have confirmed.

We sold the Estate in its entirety to New City Estates and not in single units as your letter seems to imply. Your comment re. mailing lists etc. is not how we conduct our affairs at Irish Life. I therefore return your postal order.

Yours sincerely,

Gerry Danaher

**GERRY DANAHER,
GENERAL MANAGER,
PLANNING & COMMUNICATIONS.**

Registered in Ireland number 152576
Registered office: Irish Life Centre, Dublin 1

Directors: Conor McCarthy (Chairman),
David Kingston (Managing),
James Anderson, Neville Bowen (U.K.),
David Davies (U.K.), Michael Donnelly,
Brian Duncan, Richard Howlin, Patrick Kenny,
Patrick Kilroy, John McCarrick,
Tomás Ó Cofaigh, Marie O'Connor

Salem Court
Maxwell Road
Dublin 6

24 September 1993

Mr Jerry Danaher
General Manager
Planning and Communications
Irish Life Assurance plc
Irish Life Centre
Lower Abbey Street
Dublin 1

Dear Jerry,

You are so correct. Of course Lisney were right. But I never implied
that I only wanted to buy one of the apartments – I am of means, sir,
and capable of raising a consortium.

However, I am glad to see that you have given up the law – I have never
trusted a man in a wig myself. I trust that you are finding insurance
and property just as lucrative, added to which you can have a few jars
without the media hyena pack hot on your heels.

Sadly my eldest, Tobias, has his heart set on a career at the bar and
I was wondering, Mr Danaher, if you would consider selling me your old
wig and gown to present to him? I enclose a £5 down payment in case someone
else makes a counter offer.

Yours sincerely,

John Mackay

Mr John Mackay

Mr Jerry Danaher
General Manager
Planning and Communications
Irish Life Assurance plc
Irish Life Centre
Lower Abbey Street
Dublin 1

Salem Court
Maxwell Road
Dublin 6

12 October 1993

Dear Jerry,

I wrote to you on September 24 enclosing £5 as a down payment for your wig and gown to present to my son Tobias.

I have yet to receive a reply. What's the problem?

If the fiver wasn't enough, here's another.

If they're not for sale, please tell me.

Failing that, we'll drop in next Monday and Tobias can try them on. We'll arrive about 11.30, and we can wait as long as we have to until you're free to see us.

Yours sincerely,

John Mackay

Mr John Mackay

Irish Life

Irish Life Assurance plc
Irish Life Centre,
Lower Abbey Street,
Dublin 1, Ireland

Telephone 01 704.2000
Telex 32562 / Fax 704.1908

15th October 1993

Mr. John Mackay,

Salem Court,
Maxwell Road,
DUBLIN 6

Dear Mr. Mackay,

Thank you for your letters dated 24 September and 12th October, addressed to Mr. Jerry Danaher..

I do not understand your letter - I can only assume that you have sent this letter to the wrong person. Mr. Gerry Danaher, our Asst. General Manager, Planning and Communications is **not** a Solicitor.

I return your £5 postal order and £5 note herewith, together with your stamped addressed envelopes.. It is, therefore, not necessary for you to call in to this office on Monday as suggested in your letter.

Yours sincerely,

Maureen Kenrick
Maureen Kenrick
Secretary to Gerry Danaher
AGM - PLANNING & COMMUNICATIONS

Salem Court
Maxwell Road
Dublin 6

5 October 1993

Sultan Sir Muda Hasanal
Bolkiah Mu'izuddin Waddaulah, H.M.,
D.K., D.S.P.N.B., P.S.N.B.,
P.S.L.J., S.P.B.M., P.A.N.B.,
Sultan of Brunei,
Prime Minister of Brunei,
Sovereign and Chief of Royal Orders
instituted by Sultans of Brunei,
Istana Darul Hana, Brunei,
c/o The Aviary, Osterley, England

Dear Sultan,

This is my third request that you donate thirty billion punts to the
Irish government. Not only am I no better off, but I am actually down
a tenner with zilch to show for it.

As this commercial success ratio mirrors that of the Irish economy,
you will at least by now understand why I was asking you for the money
in the first place.

Yours sincerely,

John Mackay

Mr John Mackay

PS What the heck - here's another fiver.

Salem Court
Maxwell Road
Dublin 6

Cllr Gay Mitchell TD
Lord Mayor of Dublin
Mansion House
Dublin 2

17 Feb 1993

Dear Cllr Mitchell,

Well done on your elevation to the high office of first citizen, keeping up the family tradition - I have had the pleasure of voting for Jim in the past. What a laugh, though, that you became Lord Mayor through the votes of just two other people on the six-strong Fine Gael Councillor's group. I am sure you would prefer if the post was directly elected by the people you represent so capably.

However, the elitist nature of the current system does give the mayoralty an essence of royalty - and, speaking of royalty, soon may She follow Her Daughter to Dublin, as you have so courageously suggested, letting you thumb your nose at the orange neandarthals who recently insulted you in your trip to "foreign" Belfast!

But to the point. I hope you can help me to help a niece of mine, who is currently working on a UCD thesis with the rather academic title of "Politics And People - Electoral Interaction In The Multiple Seat STV System". She has asked me for amusing "anecdotes" to illustrate the impact of our system on the valuable time of national legislators. One springs to mind concerning your good self, the authenticity of which I felt it appropriate to confirm "from the horse's mouth".

A friend of mine who served with you on the Dublin City VEC some years ago tells me of a controversial debate which he believed could land him in hot water whichever way he voted.

You imaginatively decided to verbally abuse a Fianna Fail Councillor at the meeting, consistently calling him a "Fianna Fail hack" and "Charlie's little hack" every time he spoke. When another Fianna Fail member intervened, you told him he was "nothing but a hack as well" - and kept up your torrent of peurile abuse until the chairman was forced to ask you to withdraw from the meeting. This you did - and left before the vote was taken!

I would be glad if you would allow my niece to include this amusing, yet informational, anecdote in her thesis.

Yours sincerely,

John Mackay

Mr John Mackay

PS Congratulations on bringing the Olympics and Mother Teresa to Dublin.

Teach an Ard–Mhaoir,
Baile Atha Cliath 2,
Eire
Telefon: 761845, 712402
Fax: 6796573

The Rt. Hon. The Lord Mayor Alderman Gay Mitchell, T.D.

Mansion House
Dublin 2
Ireland
Telephone: 761845, 712402
Fax: 6796573

2nd March, 1993.

Mr. John MacKay,

Salem Court,
Maxwell Road,
Dublin 6.

Dear Mr. MacKay,

Many thanks indeed for your interesting letter, and thank you also for your kind comments and good wishes.

I wish your niece well with her thesis and whilst the story you outline is an interesting one, I am afraid that there is no truth in it and it should therefore not be used.

With best wishes.

Yours sincerely,

LORD MAYOR OF DUBLIN

GM/CS

Salem Court
Maxwell Road
Dublin 6

Mr Gay Byrne
c/o RTE Television
Donnybrook, Dublin 4

26 June 1993

Dear Gay,

You must have been angered by the trauma of being dragged through the courts like a criminal, and by the outrageous judicial claim that your viewers pay little attention to you. The scandal has spurred my wife Dympna and I to write to let you know how much you mean to us.

However, while you are a person to whom anyone can unburden themselves and not feel embarrassed, we implore you NOT TO READ THIS OUT: while becoming less inhibited, we nevertheless feel our secret cannot be shared with anyone but you.

Gay, ever since Dympna and I shyly cuddled in front of the Late Late show to round off our very first date so many happy years ago, you have been "Our Presenter" in the way that other couples have "Their Song". We now want to tell you about our most precious and intimate moments, a weekly affair that is part of our lives — our Friday night date with desire.

Each Friday we send our youngest, Suzie, to her aunt Mary's for the night, and we insist that Tobias, our student son, go to a disco or visit a video game arcade, or anything. But on no account is he to come home before midnight — and he must be gone from the house by nine!

As the nine o'clock news is running, we get undressed upstairs after pulling the curtains, locking the doors and turning up the central heating. Just as that disembodied American voice says, "Ladies and Gentlemen, to whom it concerns..." we curl up before the fire, naked, just as the first men and women must have done in caves.

As we watch, we clip the savings coupons off food packaging, occasionally volunteering our opinions when you have a controversial debate. Come 11.30, we always joke to you on the TV: "Gay, we've a coupon for 10p off a packet of fig rolls for everyone in the audience."

There is no harm done and, before the trauma of your court case spurred us to write this letter, it was a secret we shared with no-one. Now, at last, you know: Gay Byrne, welcome to our world.

Gay, everybody you meet must be looking for something, but fear not, we seek nothing — save a signed photograph. Please! There's a fiver enclosed to cover the cost; if there is anything left over, please give it to your audience fund for the poor black and white babies.

Yours sincerely,

John Mackay

Mr John Mackay

for John & Dympna

With love

Gay Byrne

LATE LATE SHOW AUDIENCE TICKETS

Thank you for your request for LATE LATE SHOW audience tickets and we have pleasure in enclosing same. If it should happen that you are not available to attend on that date <u>we would be grateful if you would ensure</u> that the tickets are used, or returned to us, as there is a long waiting list for tickets.

The programme is one in which the audience is <u>invited and expected</u> to join in. We would ask you to bear this in mind when you come.

If you would like to do a "Rap", sing "hello" or recite a "Limerick" - please make yourself known to Maura Connolly when she comes out to talk to the audience prior to the show.

May we take this opportunity to thank you for your interest in the programme and for taking the trouble to write.

Yours sincerely,

Siobhán Hoare

SIOBHAN HOARE
LATE LATE SHOW

P.S. Ticket request per *Gay Byrne*

RADIO TELEFÍS ÉIREANN Dublin 4 Ireland Telephone 01 643111 Telex 93700 Fax 643098. Baile Átha Cliath Éire Teiefon 01 643111 Teleics 93700 Fax 643096.

FRIDAY 15th OCTOBER '93
STUDIO ONE AT 9.15 p.m.

Doors Open: 8.15 p.m.
Doors Close: 8.30 p.m.

№ 004

ADMIT ONE
COMPLIMENTARY

Persons under 16 years not admitted.

FRIDAY 15th OCTOBER '93
STUDIO ONE AT 9.15 p.m.

Doors Open: 8.15 p.m.
Doors Close: 8.30 p.m.

№ 003

ADMIT ONE
COMPLIMENTARY

Persons under 16 years not admitted.

Mr Gay Byrne
c/o RTE Television
Donnybrook
Dublin 4

Salem Court
Maxwell Road
Dublin 6

12 October 1993

Dear Gay,

Many thanks indeed for the signed photo - and the lovely surprise of two tickets for the Late Late Show!

After much soul-searching, Dympna and I have concluded that attending in person would break the spell of many years watching the show from the security of our sitting room. Also, as we always watch the show naked, we might cause a commotion if we turned up in the flesh!

We had thought of asking you to read us a secret rhyme on the air - "I'd like to say a big hello to Dympna and to John who every Friday watch the Late Late Show with nothing on" - but then we thought that it might cause a re-run of the "Bishop And The Nightie" incident, so maybe best not bother.

Anyway, Gay, thanks again for everything, and here's another fiver for your audience black and white babies fund.

Yours sincerely,

John Mackay

Mr John Mackay

Salem Court
Maxwell Road
Dublin 6

Dr Anthony Clare
St. Patrick's Hospital
James' Street
Dublin 8

24 September 1993

Dear Professor Clare,

I seek your help with a delicate family matter which principally concerns my wife Dympna's mother, Maisie. She has a heart of gold: alas, age and alcohol have taken their toll. After living with us for years, she has recently found solace in a privately run refuge for the elderly bewildered.

We now share our home with Toby, our son, a 22-year-old student, who practices on his slide trombone for two hours every evening, and Susie, our adolesecent daughter who appears to have joined "the screamers", a sect whose dominant philosophy involves yelling at parents. When we finish our evening meal, just as, I imagine, other families are passing around the After Eights, if Toby is practising his scales and Susie is "expressing anger", the MacKay home is Bedlam revisited.

Here's the rub: Maisie, who plays the tin whistle and does an impromptu vaudeville routine involving disgusting jokes she heard from a sailor in Belfast in early 1955, wants to leave the refuge and come back to live with us. Professor Clare, I am not an unreasonable man, but, stricken by guilt about her mum, Dympna agrees with Maisie. I am married to a "Dympnomaniac". Do you do house calls?

We have all heard your programme on Radio 4, "In The Psychiatrist's Chair", and if I was to persuade Dympna to participate with you — as though it were a "party game", I'm sure you could end up with Maisie remaining where she — and we — are happiest: living separate lives. The alternative doesn't bear thinking about: putting Maisie "In The Psychiatrist's Chair" — and connecting it to 220 volts!

I enclose £5 towards any immediate expenses involved.

Yours sincerely,

John Mackay

Mr John Mackay

St. Patrick's Hospital

P.O. BOX No. 136, JAMES'S ST., DUBLIN 8.
TELEPHONE: 677 5423. FAX: 679 8865.

ST. EDMUNDSBURY,
LUCAN, CO. DUBLIN.
TELEPHONE: 628 0221.

PSYCHIATRIC UNIT,
ST. JAMES'S HOSPITAL,
DUBLIN. TEL: 537941.

PROF. ANTHONY W. CLARE
M.D. F.R.C.P.I., F.R.C.Psych, M.Phil.,
MEDICAL DIRECTOR.

1st October, 1993.

Mr. John Mackay,

Salem Court,
Maxwell Road,
Dublin 6.

Dear Mr. Mackay,

Thank you for your letter of the 24th September, 1993. I am somewhat flattered by your invitation to act as a sort of go-between between yourselves and your mother-in-law, but I am afraid that this is one invitation I will have to turn down! From what you have to say in your interesting letter someone has to tell Maisie that it is best that she stays where she is. I think this is something that, for example, a good general practitioner should be able to do or indeed the family itself. I note however that your wife is not so sure that her mother should stay where she is and I take it that is where the difficulty arises. Until therefore you and your wife have sorted out this situation I don't feel myself that I can be of very much help.

I thank you for your letter and I return the postal order.

Very best wishes,

Yours sincerely,

Anthony W. Clare, MD.

Salem Court
Maxwell Road
Dublin 6

24 September 1993

Mr Tim O'Connor
Head of Sport
RTE
Donnybrook
Dublin 4

Dear Mr O'Connor,

Although RTE's coverage of minority sport has improved enormously in recent years, inevitably, some worthwhile sports are ignored.

Mr O'Connor, John MacKay is a pigeon fancier. I make no apologies for my lifelong love of the working man's sport of kings.

You have probably never given much thought to pigeon racing or even known any fanciers. Our lot are seldom in the saloons and restaurants of fashionable Dublin.

Anyway, here's the plan. You introduce a regular slot on the Sunday Sports programme. I will act as anchor. The title for this show within a show: Pigeon Notes by Lofty. I am not particularly tall, but the pun on pigeons' palaces will raise a knowing smile on fanciers everywhere. Private jokes on public television are okay provided, say, you don't ask Charlie Bird to present the programme.

Pigeon Notes would let RTE innovate the presentation of a new sport. I suppose that 2FM Eye In The Sky helicopter is free after breakfast, so it would be useful for close-ups of the birds in flight. Sponsors would probably demand logos on the pigeons, so you could let me know what is acceptable on this front.

I look forward to hearing from you.

Yours sincerely,

John Mackay

Mr John Mackay

Dublin 4, Ireland
Telephone 01 643111
Telex 30649
Telefax 643032

Baile Átha Cliath 4, Éire
Telefón 01 643111
Teleics 30649
Telefax 643032

Radio Telefís Éireann
Sports Department

28th September 1993

Mr. John MacKay

Salem Court
Maxwell Road
Dublin 6

Dear John, (or may I call you Lofty?)

Thank you for your brilliant proposal on Pigeon racing (Now,
why didn't I think of that?)

There are a few details to be considered before proceeding -
like the use of a glider rather than the eye-in-the-sky
chopper (for some reason or other, pigeons don't fancy
flying alongside helicopters - jealousy, I presume). Also,
because of the shortage of space afforded by your average
gickna, sponsorship is a problem, unless the bird can be
persuaded to trail a fifty-foot banner in its wake extolling
the virtues of, say, Maxwell House, or even Maxwell Road where,
I bet, the air must be pretty thin at times.

Yours sincerely

Tim O'Connor
Group Head, TV Sport

Salem Court
Maxwell Road
Dublin 6

2 March 1993

Emmett Stagg TD
Minister of State for the Environment
Leinster House
Dublin 2

Dear Mr Stagg,

From the high vantage point of long-awaited power, you're slamming the door on the local authority housing mess - a scandalously well-funded white elephant, and I am glad to see that you, Mr Stagg, are taking the bull by the horns.

Never mind the petty begrudgers who attack you for employing your daughter and cousin. As you say, if you were indulging in nepotism, you would have employed your wife's cousin as well. Anyway, is the family not the building block on which our Constitution is rooted? When I was in business, my wife Dympna made the tea while my son Toby and daughter Suzie packed the envelopes. Bottom line - food on our table. Why should the Stagg household starve?

Okay, so your family are paid by the taxpayers. Okay, so you would have opposed this in the Marxist manifestation of your distant past. However, as they say, previously you were not as wise as you are now. Those not lucky enough to be members of your family may whinge, but the people voted for change, and you have changed. Change is progress. Progress is good. Well done.

Having recently returned from abroad, I am considering joining the Labour Party. When I left a decade ago, it was Garret the Good versus Charlie the Bad - nice at last to see Dick the Enigma enter the frame. No longer need Labour wait, nor their families (just a joke!).

So here's the point of my letter. My family were of Newbridge some time ago, and I may be moving to Kildare within the year. I would appreciate some local advice - what areas of Kildare are wise investments at the moment? Perhaps one of your cousins may be in real estate - do send them my way.

Yours sincerely,

John Mackay

Mr John Mackay

PS I too am a socialist - but socialism isn't about pulling someone down when they become a TD and help out their own. It's about bringing everyone up to the same level, and you've got to start somewhere.

OIFIG AN AIRE STÁIT AG AN ROINN COMHSHAOIL
(Office of the Minister of State at the Department of the Environment)

BAILE ÁTHA CLIATH I
(Dublin I)

10 March, 1993

Mr. John Mackay

Salem Court
Maxwell Road
Dublin 6

Dear Mr. Mackay

I have received your letter of 2 March, 1993 and I want to thank you for your kind good wishes and support.

As regards areas of Kildare in which to invest at the moment, I would suggest that you talk directly to Mr. Noel Finn in Kildare County Council. He is the County Development Officer and you can write to him at the Council's Offices at St. Mary's, Naas, Co. Kildare.

Best wishes for the future.

Yours sincerely,

Emmet M. Stagg T.D.
Minister of State

Salem Court
Maxwell Road
Dublin 6

3 June 1993

Emmet Stagg TD
Minister of State for the Environment
Leinster House
Dublin 2

Dear Mr Stagg,

I wrote to you some months ago about my impending move to Kildare, and asked you to point me towards a cousin of yours in real estate. You suggested a Mr Finn who, it now appears, IS NOT RELATED TO YOU IN ANY WAY and does not even appear to be in the real estate business.

I'm afraid I rather put my foot in it in this context with the Kildare County Manager, which caused some embarrassment to myself and my wife Dympna. I have since apologised to the Manager, a Mr Lyons (is he a relation?), who is a model of professionalism and integrity.

Should the topic arise in hostile manner, please feel free to blame me for any misunderstandings – I understand that it is the done thing in these circumstances that the fellow least in the public eye is deemed to be most "expendible". Seems sensible enough.

Yours sincerely,

John Mackay

Mr John Mackay

PS It shows you are right, though, Emmet... break the family circle, etc. But try telling that to the cold-blooded policemen of political correctness, who would try to herd all Stagg cousins, uncles and antlers out of the boardroom!

PPS Well done on your performance so far in government. Both yourself and Michael D, through the pragmatic integrity of your post-Berlin Wall socialism, have confounded the visionless critics who prematurely consigned you to perpetual opposition. I enclose a token donation to put towards your next election campaign.

PPPS In the circumstances, should I continue to follow up the house business with Mr Finn, or would it be more sensitive to shift to another agent?

OIFIG AN AIRE STÁIT AG AN ROINN COMHSHAOIL
(Office of the Minister of State at the Department of the Environment)

BAILE ÁTHA CLIATH I
(Dublin I)

24 June, 1993

Mr. John Mackay,

Salem Court,
Maxwell Road,
Dublin 6.

Dear John,

I have received your letter of 3 June, 1993 and I am grateful
for your strong support. I would advise you to pursue the
matter of the house with Mr. Finn.

I am returning your postal order and I hope you will not take
offence in this regard. I greatly appreciate your kind offer
of support, but I do not accept individual donations. If you
wish to contribute to the Labour Party you can send the Postal
Order to Ray Kavanagh, General Secretary, Labour Party, 16
Gardiner Place, Dublin 1.

Yours sincerely,

Emmet M. Stagg, T.D.
Minister of State

Salem Court
Maxwell Road
Dublin 6

6 October 1993

Fr Pat Buckley
The Oratory
Princes Gardens
Larne
County Antrim
Northern Ireland

Dear Fr Buckley,

I wrote to you last February seeking natural contraceptive guidance for my clerical adultery group, and you helpfully suggested an old Celtic potion which you got from a rural Archdeacon. We've been imbibing the brew ever since! Did you know it is also hallucinegenic if taken in larger quantities than the specified two teaspoons?

I store my supply in the fridge and, yesterday morning, distracted by radio reports of the new Papal Encyclical, I poured your potion by mistake onto the family cornflakes instead of the milk.

Within moments, our eldest, Tobias, who had turned into a tropical toadstool, was being chased round the kitchen table by our daughter Susie on an elderly antelope, while my wife Dympna had sprouted wings and a halo and was singing soprano while tap dancing in the sink, accompanied on matching harps by the Pope and the Rev Ian Paisley.

The trip went bad when Dympna's mother, Maisie, insisted on eating everyone else's cornflakes until, to the tune of the music from "Jaws", she exploded across the kitchen like the fat diner who ate a wafer-thin mint too many in Monty Python's "Meaning of Life".

Father Buckley, I must now replenish my supply of the brew, which gives rise to another problem with which I hope you can help. As you know, the recipe specifies the hind legs of a hare caught in March. This caught me flak from the Animals Rights lot, but I knew I was on theologically sound ground when I took advice from a coursing cleric.

More urgently, Father Buckley, as the hare must be caught in March and as it is now October, what do I do for the next six months?

Yours sincerely,

John Mackay

Mr John Mackay

PS As the concoction includes only natural ingredients, is it approved by Veritates Splendor or is it defined as a dissident dose?

THE ORATORY
Princes Gardens,
Larne,
Co. Antrim,
Northern Ireland
BT40 1RQ

Fr. Pat Buckley

13 / 10 / 93

Dear John,

Thank you for your letter of Oct 6th. I was very taken with your description of the family breakfast scene. It confirmed my suspicions that you and yours are deeply spiritual, highly intelligent and gifted beyond understanding.

The side effects you describe are to be expected in the first instance. When I first took the potion I discovered I was able to fly (in the dark only) and I had visits at 3 a.m. from Gandhi, St Basil the Great, Bishop Carroll of Dublin (RIP), and a number of other lesser personages. I was also able to visit friends in Limbo and Purgatory.

I'm sorry for your lack of March hare. I enclose some dried March hare for your use and some tablets made from the womb lining of the armadillo bird - for use only if the the attacks get too bad.

With best wishes,
Your humble servant,

Pat Buckley

An Taoiseach
Albert Reynolds TD
Oifig an Taoiseach
Government Buildings
Dublin 2

Salem Court
Maxwell Road
Dublin 6

5 October 1993

Dear Albert,

Summer is gone, Dympna's cold has cleared up, and the kids are out from under our feet. Unlike the Reynolds', the Mackays did not go abroad this year, so you can't call us fair weather friends! But down to business – here's a one-page update on the dog-bowl project.

Kieran and Colm at the IDA and Alan McCarthy at Bord Trachtala have been more than helpful in sniffing out market research. They seem happy with the brand name – the Irish Wolf-It-Down-Hound Bowl – which we're ready to register with Dublin Castle. And so it's all systems go, with our first ad campaign starting next week!

Now to a sensitive matter, Albert. As Taoiseach, it would clearly be tricky for you to be seen to endorse a commercial product.

However, I presume there would be no problem with ads that included a small photo of yourself and said "this unique all-Irish product is the outcome of a commercial viability study instigated by an Taoiseach, Mr Albert Reynolds TD - so buy it today".

Anyway, once it's in the papers, there's nothing anyone can do - and if the PD puritanical police make an issue of it, you can say you knew nothing and we'll just apologise and give a few quid to charity!

So, unless we hear to the contrary by next Wednesday, we'll start sending the ads to the papers.

Yours sincerely,

John Mackay

Mr John Mackay

PS Again, many thanks for your assistance in instigating this unique commercial venture.

PPS Do you think young Philip at C&D Pet Foods would go for a Wolf-It-Down-Hound-Bowl joint venture with Max Dog-nosh?

PPPS Here's another fiver for the party!

Salem Court
Maxwell Road
Dublin 6

24 September 1993

Mary Robinson
President of Ireland
Aras an Uachtaran
Phoenix Park
Dublin

Dear President,

I am planning a surprise anniversary evening out for my wife Dympna in the second week in November - and, your excellency, I want to make it a night to remember for both of us.

As Dympna has always been a great admirer of yourself and Steven Spielberg, I'd like to treat her to an evening viewing (8.30 showing) of Jurassic Park, in the best seats at a premier cinema, seated beside the President of Ireland and her husband.

Afterwards we could have a light supper in our house or, if you prefer, in one of the new restaurants in the Temple Bar area.

And you'll not have to put your hand in your pocket all evening: John Mackay will pay for everything.

I hope you can oblige, and I look forward to hearing from you.

Yours sincerely,

John Mackay

Mr John Mackay

PS Is there any chance of a signed photo? I enclose £5 to cover any administrative costs.

OIFIG RÚNAÍ AN UACHTARÁIN
BAILE ÁTHA CLIATH 8

OFFICE OF THE SECRETARY TO THE PRESIDENT
DUBLIN 8

8 October, 1993

Dear Mr. Mackay,

The President, Mary Robinson, has asked me to thank you most
sincerely for your very kind invitation to her to dinner on the
occasion of your wedding anniversary in November 1993.

The President greatly appreciated your thoughtfulness in extending
the invitation to her but regrets that, due to the extent of her
existing commitments, at that time, she is unable to accept.

She sends her very best wishes to you and your wife on this happy
occasion.

Yours sincerely,

Joseph Brennan
Deputy Secretary to the President

Mr. John Mackay.